Forces of Character

By:

Chad Hennings

with

Jon Finkel

FORCES OF CHARACTER

Conversations About Building A Life Of Impact

Published in the United States by Chad Hennings

C-Force Publishing

ISBN 978-0-9909649-1-9

eBook ISBN 978-0-9909649-2-6

www.ForcesOfCharacter.com

First Edition

Cover Design: Chris Hobrecker

Editor: Jared Evans

Back Cover Photo Credit: Brenna Hennings

DEDICATION

To Chase and Brenna:

This book is a reminder that everyday you have a choice as to the person you choose to be.

CONTENT

INTRODUCTION   6

CHAPTER 1   Roger Staubach   22

CHAPTER 2   Tom Henricks   41

CHAPTER 3   Virginia Prodan   68

CHAPTER 4   Justice Clarence Thomas   92

CHAPTER 5   Bob Sweeney   111

CHAPTER 6   Dr. Edith Eva Eger   137

CHAPTER 7   Carey Casey   152

CHAPTER 8   Jason Garrett   173

CHAPTER 9   Gregg Popovich   198

CHAPTER 10 Troy Aikman   224

EPILOGUE   246

INTRODUCTION

I stole football cards from a little girl.

When I reach back into the depths of my memory to try to pinpoint the exact moment when I had a sense of what it meant to have character, or at least to know the difference between right and wrong, my mind settles on that one memory: the time in second grade when I stole football cards from a little girl.

I was staying at a buddy's house for a sleepover and his younger sister had a stack of football cards in her room. I also collected football cards, and back then I was a huge Minnesota Vikings fan. Their biggest star in that era was quarterback Fran Tarkenton, and his card was one of the few Vikings cards I didn't have. As I flipped through her deck I saw it: a mint-condition Tarkenton card staring right at me—and oh man, did I want it.

My friend found a few cards in her stack that he wanted as well, and instead of asking her for them or offering her a trade for them, we just decided to take them. I don't recall much hesitation about that decision—until later that night when I heard his sister crying to her dad that some of her cards were missing.

It was one of those significant emotional events that I felt in both my head and my gut. I remember thinking, *This little girl is crying and it's all my fault.*

I probably didn't know the word for it at the time, but I'll never forget the feeling: it was guilt, and I couldn't take it. As bad as I wanted that Fran Tarkenton card, I admitted that I stole it and gave it back. The card wasn't worth the awful feeling that was growing inside of me.

My friend's father made me tell my dad about what we did when I got home, and let's just say I was disciplined accordingly. My dad held me accountable for the action of stealing. I didn't understand it right away since I had already given the card back, but now I realize my dad was helping me calibrate my moral compass; or to use a phrase from my days as a fighter pilot in the Air Force, he put me on the proper vector. Having the proper vector is just as important in life as it is in aviation.

To illustrate this, consider a person's life as a high-performance jet. The jet operates at the cutting edge of physics, where every decision made by the pilot is critical, and even small choices can have major consequences. Now imagine that in the midst of a flight the pilot makes a series of calculations and concludes that he must make a rapid ascent. He pulls back on his stick expecting to rocket into the stratosphere, but instead he impacts the ground. Catastrophe.

So what happened?

Simple. The pilot was flying upside-down.

Forces of Character

Here's how: Through a series of in-flight decisions the pilot had been flying upside-down for quite some time, so when the moment came to increase his altitude, he pulled back on his stick to ascend without checking his vector. Improper vector, Improper direction. Rather than hitting the sky, he hit the earth. This scenario is much more plausible than you may think.

A person's life is the same. An individual can be born with the strength, talent, brains, charisma and power to accomplish anything they want, but if their vector is off and they don't maintain a constant sense of who they are and where they want to go, there will be unintended consequences with poor outcomes.

Young men and women need people in their lives to put them on the proper vector, to help them find their moral compass; because as they find their way in this world, they're going to push the envelope to determine what actions they're willing to tolerate from themselves, and also what those around them are willing to tolerate.

In the story involving the football card I was swiftly reprimanded for what I did, and I learned two things: one, I shouldn't steal; and two, I possessed an inner moral compass that I didn't quite yet know how to read.

Enter: My brother.

***

I grew up on a farm, which means I saw the quintessential All-American work ethic from my parents and grandparents on a daily basis. It was my older brother, however, who taught me the value of holding myself to a higher standard and expecting more of myself. He did this as only an older brother could, through equal parts fun and torture.

The fun parts involved lifting weights and running routes with my brother, who was the quarterback of the football team. I was the tight end. The torture parts meant being dragged outside to practice at all hours: early morning, afternoon, late at night, it didn't matter. And at the time I always resisted.

I know people see me now as a fighter pilot and an ex-pro football player, but back then I was very hesitant when it came to physicality. I don't know if it was fear of failure or if I felt like I wasn't the Rambo type, but the fact is I needed to be dragged along. To this day, I'm grateful he forced my hand.

I admired my brother so much because he was a great athlete, and he was also the hardest worker on the team. Of course, he had me running routes in the hot sun until I puked, and he just stood in the shade and threw to me, but that's where I began to understand what work ethic truly was—in a mental sense and in a physical sense.

Over the course of the summer leading into my sophomore year, as my brother dragged me into the weight room to get our reps up, or out to the field to run the entire route tree until I keeled over, something started to happen. I could feel the strength coming on with the weights I lifted; I noticed the speed that I now possessed when I ran with my teammates. It was empowering. The training, which I had to be forced into, became a part of me, and by mimicking my brother's actions I started to see personal success. And I owned it.

Those few years when my brother and I overlapped in high school forged a bedrock work ethic in me that would continue throughout my high school, college and professional careers. Still, my inner fortitude and character was constantly tested.

Case in point: the time I got my butt handed to me on the wrestling mat.

***

I wrestled my freshman year of high school but I wasn't mature enough then to cut the weight I needed to, and I wasn't fully committed. I decided to try basketball my sophomore year but I just didn't have a passion for it, which led me back to wrestling my junior year.

By that time I had grown physically and I could skate by on natural size and strength. I ended up making it to the state tournament where I lost to a guy I was clearly better than. I was totally deflated and felt like a failure. Shortly after that, I entered a freestyle wrestling tournament to try to get back on the winning track.

I remember staring across the mat at a guy I knew deep down I should mop the floor with, but as soon as the match started I was in trouble. He was more confident. He moved with purpose. He was in my head right away.

Needless to say, I got my butt kicked. Again.

I was devastated.

I spent a lot of time after that thinking about the kind of person and competitor I wanted to be. Was I the kind of guy who accepted failure or the kind who learned from it? Was failure going to bring me down or build me up? After much inner turmoil and self-reflecting on my performance, I made a conscious choice, a vow to myself, that has stayed with me to this day: I will never be outworked.

Once I made up my mind I was empowered by a sense of purpose. I committed to becoming stronger than everyone I competed against. I was going to bust my butt to be faster, quicker and more tenacious. I began building upon the foundational aspect of my work ethic and who I truly was.

As is often the case, the harder I worked the more confident I became. I also began to use positive visualization, a strategy where I envisioned success and positive outcomes in my mind before a game or contest.

I would close my eyes and run through all of my plays on the football field or work through all of my wrestling moves on the mat. By the time my senior year rolled around I thought of myself as an unstoppable force—and on the wrestling mat, I was. I beat every wrestler I faced that season by at least eight points. I pinned almost everyone and won the state championship.

More important than the winning, however, was the fact that my mindset and my work ethic were validated by the results I was getting.

Looking back on that time in my life, I can't imagine where I would be if I had let that butt kicking affect me negatively. I also couldn't imagine where I would be without having been blessed with positive influences in my life like my brother. In fact, from high school to the Air Force Academy to the Dallas Cowboys and in my business and personal relationships, I have made a conscious choice to surround myself with people of high character.

In many ways, this book is a culmination of those choices. In highlighting what character means to personal mentors like Roger Staubach, leaders I've played with like Troy Aikman, men who have influenced my thinking like U.S. Supreme Court Justice Clarence Thomas, among others, I hope to help readers develop character within themselves and learn to identify it within other people.

This is not an easy thing to do because character isn't a zero sum game. It's not stagnant and it's not just a moment in time. People don't have it one day and then lack it the next. Character is, by its very nature, kinetic.

***

Let the following words sink in.

Character. Is. Kinetic.

It is a living, breathing thing inside of you that evolves over time, and the first step in that evolution, whether you end up being a person of high character or not, begins with a choice. People don't simply wake up one morning and decide to rob a bank, just as they don't roll out of bed one day and open a homeless shelter. Each action is the end result of thousands of tiny choices being made every day by an individual throughout their lives; and all of those decisions are guided by a moral compass, proving that what we do today matters tomorrow, even if tomorrow feels like an eternity from where we want to eventually be.

That's why character is kinetic. Right up until a person reaches what I like to call the "rocking chair moment" of life, in their last days, they can look back on how they've lived and still choose who they want to be.

And since character is kinetic, it also has momentum, both positive and negative.

If someone can establish a habit of making high-character decisions in their life, positive things tend to happen. If they consistently make poor decisions, negative things tend to happen. The question at hand then becomes this:

How does someone train to consistently act with character?

And by "train" I mean that people can exercise their behavior just as they'd exercise a muscle. Character isn't something people can expect to turn on like a light switch. And if they think they can do that, they'll fail. I promise.

That is why I am writing this book. Too often when people speak or write about character it becomes a one-off event. They point to an intriguing quote or showcase someone with character, but they are leaving out the most important part—the transformational piece.

Rather than point to someone and say, "they have character," I want to dig a little deeper. What was the transformational moment in this person of character's life that caused them to live a life of high integrity? Who did they look up to at that moment? Who helped them? How did they stumble along the way? How did they pick themselves up and overcome adversity? What are their day-to-day challenges? How did they finish? These are the things that are most important.

But before someone can answer any of those questions, they had to have a moment (or several moments) of clarity that forced them to think about who they are, who they want to be and where they want to go.

I call this the foundational phase.

This is the portion of self-discovery in which a person establishes a foundation and a vision of who they are as a person. It's that moment when people understand that someone is looking up to them, or counting on them, or watching them on a daily basis for guidance. It's that period of recognition when a person understands that their actions, thoughts and words all have consequences far beyond their own lives, stretching into their families and their communities. In short, this is when a person establishes their vector, when they stop thinking about the past or about what might feel good in the moment and start making decisions based on the type of person they want to be. It's when they commit to demonstrating habits of excellence, when they elevate their performance toward a noble purpose— when they begin lifting others to their highest potential.

For me, that first transformational moment was when I stole a football card, and I've had dozens of transformational moments since. These moments will be different for every reader.

Over the course of this book, I will share a series of conversations with people who I believe to be high-character individuals. Some you have heard of, others you haven't, but at some point they all experienced transformational moments in their lives and faced the same questions:

Who do I want to be? How do I want to be remembered? What steps must I take to get there?

My hope is that by reading about the following Forces of Character, you are putting yourself on the path to become one.

Chapter 1

Roger Staubach

"Having character means having a consistent positive behavior

pattern in every aspect of your life."

Roger Staubach the athlete is certainly someone to admire. He's a member of both the College and Pro Football halls of fame; He won the Heisman Trophy at the Naval Academy, and he won two Super Bowls and a Super Bowl MVP with the Dallas Cowboys.

Roger Staubach the man is even more impressive. He served his country in the Navy, he built a commercial real estate business from the ground up and became a bona fide mogul, he's been married to the same woman for 50 years and he has lived a life full of character and integrity.

But I view him as Roger Staubach the mentor. When it comes to my life, it seems whatever path I have been on Roger has been there, just twenty years further down the road than me. From being a decorated college athlete, to serving our country, to playing with the Cowboys, to running a real estate company, we have walked the same walk and we can have conversations on some very specific subjects that few others can relate to. For instance, in the modern era of the NFL, few men served in a combat zone and then went on to play professional football. That fact alone has given us a very special bond that we often talk about.

When I finally sat down to interview Roger for this book I found out that we had something else in common. After sharing my story about stealing from my friend's sister, Roger told his own story about stealing something at a very young age and how it also became a transformational moment for him in his life.

This is the perfect moment to jump into our interview:

Roger Staubach (*laughing*): I didn't steal any football cards like you, but when I was in second grade I did something similar. I went to a Catholic school, and every day on my walk home I passed a store called Gospels that sold religious goods. One day on the way home, I wandered in there and grabbed a little statue of the Blessed Virgin and took it home. I stole it, really. That night I didn't think about it too much, but the next morning I woke up, went downstairs and started crying. I can still picture it to this day—I was just sitting there on the couch crying. My mom saw me and asked what was wrong and I told her I took the statue. I remember vividly going up to my room and taking it out of the drawer that I had hidden it in to show her. I looked up at her and she said, "You need to take it back to the store right now and tell them what you did."

Chad Hennings: That must have been a long walk back.

It sure was. They didn't have any surveillance or video cameras in the stores back then so I could have gotten away with it at that point, but I walked in there and told someone who worked there that I had taken the statue and I handed it back. It was a big step for me because I knew that I was taught better than that. I've always tried to make it up to the Blessed Virgin, and that's one of the reasons I named Drew Pearson's great catch against the Vikings in the 1975 playoff game the Hail Mary pass.

And that's one of the things I want to touch upon in this book. The idea that character is really the sum of a series of choices a person makes throughout their life. So when you say you were taught better than that, who were the people in your life you looked to at an early age to help you make the right choices and to begin to form your own character?

I was fortunate that I was an only child. I had two parents who I really cared about and they cared about me, so I got off to a good start. But when I was in third grade in Catholic school there was this sister, Sister Aloysius, and she was a tough son of a gun. She believed in corporal punishment, stuff like holding books out in front of you until you started to sweat. She also knew my pain points. She made me understand the importance of studying because she wouldn't let me go on the playground until all of my work was done. She forced me into making sure that I balanced my academic life and my sports life. To this day I think about balance and I preach that to people at my company as well.

I agree that balance is hugely important, but having balance goes beyond time management, right? You need to balance your choices based on a variety of factors.

That's true. I've always tried to balance my life with what is good for me but also keeping in mind how it affects somebody else. As an athlete, that's what you learn in sports—the teamwork aspect of things—that you can't do it by yourself. I still work on it. I write things down that I don't do or that I think I can do better.

I do the same thing. Writing things down allows you to hold yourself accountable. That's an excellent habit to get into. As someone who works so hard on maintaining that balance, how do you define it? Meaning, if you're living a balanced life and everything is clicking, what does that feel like?

Some days it's a "what's in it for you day," but that's not who you want to be all the time. When you take the time to consciously put yourself in other people's shoes, however, you're going to balance your life because you're going to be taking out of life but you're going to be giving an equal amount back.

That brings up an interesting question I often think about. How do you balance your sense of empathy for someone else with your responsibility or ability to help them, especially when it comes to companies or teams? And can you instill in them a sense of moral integrity or character?

When it comes to running my company, I certainly don't go around preaching, but people who work for me adhere to two agendas: their business agenda and their personal agenda. On the business side, we want everyone to make sure their priorities are on the customers. On the personal side, I try to send a message by how I act that our business is important, but your family is more important. And they see how I live my life to back that up. This is where consistency is key. You can't say you're a person of character in one place and then not act with character in another facet of your life. People see through that. The worst thing is to preach something that you're not.

Is there someone in particular whom you either worked with or played with that you would point to as an example of having that balance, who lived a life of high character both personally and professionally?

I was fortunate to have had Coach Tom Landry as someone to look up to. When you talk about character, he was a phenomenal example of being able to be a great coach and also live a life that everyone respected. Coach Landry was a tough, hard-nosed football coach, but his strength was in his preparation. He believed that in order to succeed you had to be extremely prepared and you had to work extremely hard. That's why we won for twenty years in a row.

I was drafted by Coach Landry but never had the opportunity to play for him, unfortunately. You just mentioned how respected he was as a coach and in the community, and I think in many ways you have taken that mantle from him in Dallas, which, along with being a positive influence in my life, is one of the

reasons I wanted to interview you for Forces of Character. And this leads to my next question: So much about living a life of character is understanding that all of your actions affect other people—some positively, some negatively. Do you remember the first time you understood your ability to influence other people?

Well, I recall the first time I was told I could influence other people. What many don't know about me is that I didn't play quarterback until my senior year of high school. After my junior year, my coaches approached me and asked me if I'd be interested in switching to quarterback. When I asked them why they wanted me to do that, they said, "Because the other guys listen to you." That conversation changed my life. Those coaches, Coach Krueger and Coach McCarthy, really saw me as a quarterback, and we probably wouldn't be here talking if they hadn't.

It's amazing how the trajectory of our lives can boil down to those small moments we don't see coming. After that conversation, were you nervous? Taking over the quarterback

position of a team, on any level, is a challenge—especially starting as a senior. Did you have any doubts about your ability to lead or perform?

We had a senior quarterback named Tom Schneeman who was a freshman with me and was geared to be the senior quarterback. I worked my butt off throughout our two-a-days and I barely beat him out for the job. At the end of camp, I was told I was going to start the opening game of my senior year against Dade Chaminade. And what happened in that game is a great example of how you need other people. We were behind in the fourth quarter and I threw an off-balance pass to a player named Freddy DeFinney to win the game. I promise you, if Freddy doesn't catch that touchdown pass you'd be talking to Tom Schneeman right now because coach would have given Schneeman the start in the next game.

Unbelievable.

I really liked being a quarterback after that. Following my senior year I went to junior college at New Mexico Military Institute before I went to Navy, so by then I had two years of quarterback under my belt.

Let's talk about your time in the Navy for a bit because this is important. You and I share a similar experience of being drafted by the NFL but also having a commitment to the military to honor. You were a Heisman Trophy winner, an All-American and you had the opportunity to quarterback the Dallas Cowboys sitting right in front of you. Did you ever think about trying to get out of your commitment to the Navy? Or try to circumvent the system somehow?

This is where I can sound corny because there was no way in the world I would have ever broken my commitment to the Navy. That goes back to my mother who taught me to always live up to my commitments. They could have offered me a billion dollars and I would not have gone. I was committed to the Navy. And speaking of my mother, here's a great story. After I was drafted, Gil Brandt, who was the vice president of player personnel for the Cowboys at the time, went to my mom's house to talk to her. He made an insinuation to her that someone knew someone in Washington who might be able to get me out of my active-duty requirement—and she threw him out of the house! I'm telling that story to illustrate the kind of person my mother was. Because I was raised like that, it wasn't a thought. If I would have left the service and joined the Cowboys, I would have been trying to get out of things the rest of my life.

That's incredible. Character is usually broken down into two main parts: moral character and function character. Moral character includes self-discipline, integrity, humility and so on. That decision you made to honor your commitment is a shining example of moral character. At what point did you realize that you could still one day play in the NFL? Did you have someone in the Navy you could talk to about your long-term goals?

I had a great friend named Father Joe Ryan. Father Joe was at the Naval Academy and we were also in Vietnam together. He was wounded in Vietnam, and he kind of took me under his wing so we talked about my playing football again someday fairly often. After my third year in the service, I took two weeks leave and went to the

33

Cowboys' training camp. That's when they knew I could play because they saw that I could throw. Before I left camp Coach Landry gave me the playbook and said, "Study this. You'll be a rookie next year." I put in my resignation when I got back and completed the last year of my service. Then I joined the Cowboys.

Before we move on to your time as quarterback of the Cowboys, I want to ask you about your experience as an officer in the Navy, because that is a position of authority and that is where the traits of functional character, like work ethic, positivity and determination, can really influence other people. Are there any examples in your service time that exemplify those aspects of character and leadership, or where maybe your character was tested?

There was a situation that occurred that, to this day, I think I'm over but I'm not. I was a logistics officer in Da Nang and Chu Lai in Vietnam. I had a big responsibility because I was in charge of all the supplies coming into Chu Lai by ship. We had these landing ship tanks called LSTs and we were responsible for unloading the ships and sending the cargo to all the bases. Over time, the cargo began arriving on the bases with some of the pallets having been broken into. Of course the bases blamed it on the Navy guys. They blamed the guys who unloaded the ships, the truck loader, the driver, anyone they could, but everyone denied it. All those people were under my command.

What did you do?

I started checking everything on the ships before we did any off-loading. The first time we did it, things were broken into all over the place; this was before our guys had even been on the ship. But a few of my guys on the beach were caught in the middle of it. It was minor stuff, but some people weren't reporting what they were finding when they off-loaded stuff, which they had to do. That left it open to interpretation that they were benefitting from keeping their mouths shut.

Again, I was an officer and everyone was looking up to me. I listened to everybody's story, I heard what my chiefs had to say, but at the end of the day I had to make a decision and I had to make the right decision, because the wrong one can put fuel on the fire for people looking to undermine you or the rules. I decided then and there to reinforce my belief that you don't cut corners. I didn't want to get people in trouble, but I had to send that message and we had to discipline some of the men.

Was that difficult for you?

Oh yes.

Kind of like having to discipline a teammate, right?

Yes. It was really tough, but there's a way of doing things in life, and you just have to make sure you're an example to those who work with you or work for you. You can over-preach things, but it's really your example that counts the most. If you're going to say something you have to try to make sure you act accordingly with your directives. If you don't do that you're in trouble.

How did that idea of leading and showing character by example transfer over to your time with the Cowboys? Were you a vocal leader?

That's probably a good question to ask my teammates. I didn't preach to them to try to be a model citizen or anything; I think I simply set a good example. I played hard, I went home, I had a family, and that's what I did. It was a consistent pattern. I never got upset with anyone who had a different personal life than mine, but on the field—working, getting ready for a game, or in practice—I gave everything I had all the time. My teammates saw that. On the character side, I tried to help teammates if they wanted me to, but I didn't call anybody out for anything. There were guys who had issues and problems and I would spend time with them to help however I could. There were other players I was involved with in helping get into rehab and a lot of different things, mostly after football.

Did that mindset of showing character rather than preaching about character carry over into how you run your business as well?

Yes. When you have a company, you are responsible for these people. If there's somebody out of line you still give them another chance, but then after a while you've just got to get rid of them. They can become a cancer. That's true on a team as well. When it comes to the leadership of a team, you're still going to have the troublemakers on your team, but you can't let them be the leaders of the team. That's important. A lot of that has to do with the idea that while some players are great—great athletes—they may have almost zilch character. Most players have great character—it's a small percentage who don't.

It sounds like the idea of having character, whether you were in the Navy, on the Cowboys or running a company, came from a personal commitment to do so on a day-in and day-out basis. I think this is a concept that is very important: the idea that

character is kinetic and is the summation of thousands of choices.

That's true. I'd say that having character means having a consistent positive behavior pattern in every aspect of your life.

Exactly. It's a pattern of behavior over the course of time that defines who you are.

The toughest thing for people, myself included, is consistency. Acting with character all the time and in every instance is difficult. It might be the hardest thing there is.

Do you think you can ever fully get there?

I honestly don't know if you totally get there. All I can try to do is be consistent. That's why you have to work on balance, which we talked about earlier. Most people with character do have balance, and even though they're not perfect, they do the right things.

Amen. Thank you for your time, Roger. And thank you for being a mentor and man of character to me, personally.

I appreciate you saying that. Thank you, as well.

Chapter 2

Tom Henricks

"'Work' and 'ethic' are two words. People forget that 'ethic' is part of that phrase; that it's not just about hard work, it's about ethical work. That means being responsible for the good results and for the failures."

I'm going to assume that most people reading this book have never heard the name Tom Henricks. You've heard of his job—astronaut—and you've heard of his vehicle—the Space Shuttle—but you may not have given much thought as to what it takes to reach the top seat in all of human aviation—a Space Shuttle commander.

If Henricks were to reach the equivalent level of excellence as an NFL player he'd be a household name. People would follow him on Twitter, wear his jersey, and memorize his statistics. As a former NFL player, I remember my share of statistics too, but to me, the stats Henricks has compiled as a fighter pilot with the Air Force and as a Shuttle commander with NASA are every bit as gaudy and impressive as what Peyton Manning has accomplished on the football field.

Henricks became the first person to log more than 1,000 hours as a Space Shuttle pilot/commander. He has flown thirty-five different types of aircraft and logged more than 6,000 hours of total flying time. He has done 745 parachute jumps with a Master Parachutist rating.

That's not bad for a guy who was the first in his family to go to college and who spent his teenage years driving a tractor.

In fact, Henricks's road from humble beginnings to flying in outer space is exactly why I wanted to interview him for *Forces of Character.* To me, his achievements are the epitome of what can happen in life when you marry the All-American work ethic with a high-character individual on the proper vector. And he's one of the most down-to-earth people you'll ever listen to.

Chad Hennings: In terms of sheer pressure and unique importance, there are few jobs, if any, that can compare with being a Space Shuttle commander. To attain such an elite level of responsibility within both NASA and the government, your character has to be almost unimpeachable. You are entrusted with billions of dollars of U.S. taxpayer money and the lives of your crew in the harshest environment known to man. All that being said, every journey begins with the first step. When was the first time you remember being responsible for other people?

Tom Henricks: Let's start with this. I grew up on a farm in Ohio. Nobody in my family had ever gone to college and my first job was as a hoer for ninety cents an hour, which meant I was using a hoe to cut weeds for my grandfather. That started at about age ten. By the time I was twelve or thirteen, he gave me my first real gig. He said, "A neighbor down the road about two miles away has ten acres that he wants baled. It's too small for me, but if you want the job you can use my equipment. Also, you'll have to find your own help. It's your job if you want it." I was going to be paid like $40 or something, which was a ton of money at the time. I didn't live in that town but my cousin did, so I asked him if he had any buddies available to help with the job. I hired two of them. That was the first time I was ever in a leadership position.

And you were twelve. There's such a big difference between those times and today. I worked on a farm as well growing up, and I ran some heavy equipment at that age too. Nowadays, most parents don't allow their kids to push a lawn mower when they're ten or eleven.

Oh yeah. For that job I was driving a tractor with a baler and a wagon behind it and hired two guys who were much older than me. The challenge was that I had to manage these guys. None of us had cars so I had to figure out how to get them out there and get them home. I got the money from the guy who hired us and paid them.

Do you remember any specific lessons or things you learned from that situation in terms of influencing other people?

Absolutely. My first lesson in leadership and character was with that crew. I learned right away that you can't be lackadaisical when you're in charge. The guys working for me were townies; I didn't want them to get hurt on the wagons. I didn't want them goofing off. I had to lead by example and show them how to stack the hay on the wagons so when you go down the road it doesn't fall off.

And that was your first taste of real responsibility?

Yes, that's when I first started thinking about what it means to be a man and a leader of other men. The next significant moment for me in this regard was a couple of years later when I was the quarterback of the freshman football team. I remember during one of our games something went wrong on a play and I badmouthed one of the guys in the huddle. I mean, I really went after him. What I didn't know was that I was talking so loud that my dad heard it from the sidelines. After the game he counseled me. He said, "Never do that to one of your teammates. Never put down one of your teammates in front of the other teammates."

I argued with him, of course, saying the kid deserved it, but he said, "You don't act that way. Not if you're going to be a leader. The quarterback position is a leadership position. You've got to get your head around how you're going to present yourself to the rest of your team."

That brings us to one of the most important aspects of having character: being accountable to yourself as well as to others. Roger Staubach talked a lot about the benefits of leading by example, and your father was teaching you the same thing. Are there any other people from that stage of your life who helped mold your character?

One of the people I learned the most from was someone I never met—George Allen, the coach of the Los Angeles Rams in the 1960s. He wrote a book called *How to Train the Quarterback.* I read his book after my freshman year of high school when I learned I was going to be a varsity quarterback. The book talks about leadership in simple terms, but I think it also speaks to character. I still remember the four main rules: always be the first man on the field at practice; always be the last man off the field; know the assignment of everyone on the team; always remember that you are judged on performance. I lost the book after high school but I bought it later in life and I have a copy at home. I learned a lot from that book and the lessons from it have stayed with me.

How did the lessons in that book compare with what you actually experienced on the field? It's one thing to read about knowing the assignment of everyone on the team, but it's another to actually know everyone's assignment.

That's completely true. I really took those words to heart. I think I got to be the quarterback because I was the only guy who could remember the plays. When somebody looked at me and asked, "What am I doing on this play?" I could tell them. You've got to have enough courage and confidence in yourself. I mean, I was from a small town and I was a 130-pound football player. I remember looking at the guys in the huddle and feeling like, *I'm not going to let them down. I've got to step up so they'll follow me.* As a leader I had to be better than I thought I could be.

What's impressive to me is that at such a young age you were already seeking out people to look up to, be it in your community or through a book.

You know, I don't give my father enough credit because his influence on me was so subtle. When you live at home until you're seventeen you don't realize how much you're being influenced. I was probably fifty or fifty-five years old before I realized how big an influence he had on my life—and still does. Both he and my grandfather instilled me with a powerful work ethic. A unique aspect they talked to me about was that 'work' and 'ethic' were two words. People forget that 'ethic' is part of that phrase; that it's not just about hard work, it's about ethical work. That means being responsible for the good results and for the failures.

That's a good thing to point out. People do forget how important the 'ethic' part of that phrase is and how important work ethic is as a virtue when it comes to moral and performance excellence. You also have to make sure your energy is aimed in the right direction, or to borrow a flying term, the proper vector. Was there a defining moment in your life that clarified your purpose and commitment to what you wanted to be?

One very important event I think has defined my life. It happened when I was about thirteen and staying with my grandparents and working during the summer. I had cousins who lived in the next town and we hung out all the time. I woke up one morning after it had poured rain all night and the fields were too wet to bale hay, which meant we couldn't work outside. My cousin who was old enough to drive picked up my other cousins and went out for the day. Eventually the sun came out and they put the top down in the old convertible they were in—just four young guys with a day off of work having fun. They decided to head to Dairy Queen for an ice cream. When they pulled out of the parking lot they went around the corner on the highway and a car was stopped in the middle of the road. To avoid rear-ending the car, they swerved off the road quickly and ended up hitting a pole. Three of the guys were thrown out of the convertible and killed. They weren't wearing seat belts. Two of them were my cousins and the other one was like family. To this day, I don't know why I wasn't in that car. We did everything together. I think my grandfather had some work for me in the barn so I couldn't take the day off like those guys. Or maybe they hadn't picked me up yet.

Fate.

Fate. Something. To this day I think, *Why wasn't I in that car?* My closest buddies went to get ice cream and ended up losing their lives. I was already a Christian, but it was one of those times when you think, *How can God be so cruel as to let that happen?* That was a character changer for me because I saw grief and felt grief like I never had before. I attended three funerals in a week as a thirteen-year-old and I think I grew up right there. These were three good, wholesome, hard-working regular guys with their whole lives ahead of them. I felt that God had spared me for some purpose. I believe that one purpose was to live for them and to do things with my life that they might have dreamed of doing.

That is an incredible story. I can't fathom what must have been going through your head at that time. But when I think about it, becoming an astronaut certainly fits into the idea of doing something that young men would dream of doing.

That's true, but I didn't know I was going to be an astronaut at that point. I just knew I wanted to fly.

Where did that desire come from?

I think it came from riding the tractor for hours and hours and hours, back and forth in twenty- to forty-acre fields. I'd watch the contrails fly overhead and I became fascinated with the idea of flying. When I was twelve years old I drove my grandfather's tractor past an old grass strip airport that had a sign that said 'airplane rides $3'. So I saved up money for a week and then rode my bike two miles to the airfield. When I got there I emptied my pockets and said I wanted a ride, but the guy said it was $3 for three people, so it was actually $9 a ride. He saw my heart sink and he took me up anyway. We flew over my grandfather's farm and that was it for me. I had the bug. I knew I wanted to be a pilot. The funny thing is I never flew again until I got on an airliner to go to the Academy at Colorado Springs.

It's amazing you say that because I had such a similar experience. I had a neighbor growing up who flew a single-engine plane and he landed on a dirt road near our house sometimes. He took me for a ride when I was younger and I got that initial rush of flying. It felt like freedom.

It did. And you know, thinking of that flight to the Academy, I had an experience that has helped me keep things in perspective to this day. I remember the plane taking off and I was really upset—this was the first time I was leaving home. I was leaving my friends and family and I wouldn't see anyone again for months. All this stuff is going through my mind, and then I look across the aisle and see a guy who was a sergeant in the Army and he was fighting back tears. Eventually I found out that he was headed to Vietnam. That's when I learned that everything is relative. He was going to war and I was going to school. I had nothing to feel bad about. Changed my outlook forever.

One of the themes I'm noticing here is that you not only observe the important life moments around you, you absorb them and pull out life lessons on an ongoing basis. That fits with something I talk about in the introduction of this book, the idea that character is kinetic and is a chain of lifelong decisions. You've chosen to pull from events around you as you move through life and they have shaped your character in such a positive way. When you got to the Academy your brain must have been in overdrive. It's an environment where all your fellow classmates are strivers; they're the best of the best. You have so many opportunities and experiences to learn from. Were there any people or events that stand out as more important than the others in terms of shaping your character and career?

One big thing is that I got more out of being on the parachute team while I was there than any of the military stuff.

Why's that?

For one thing, we had real responsibility. As a cadet a lot of the stuff is just a game, but I got on the parachute team during spring break of our third class year. If I hadn't I probably wouldn't have stayed. That was enough to keep me there. It was such a kick. We were literally nineteen-year-old kids throwing other nineteen-year-old kids out of airplanes.

It's like letting an eleven-year-old kid drive a tractor.

It was. I still can't believe it. When I saw my own kids at nineteen and thought back to what I was doing at their age it was mind-boggling. It was one of those things where you give someone responsibility and they either step up or they don't. I stepped up and I loved the fact that someone gave me that responsibility.

And you ate it up.

The first jump was a ten-second freefall. We were taught the whole thing from an academic standpoint, but then you jump out of the plane and it's a whole new game. Then you do it over and over and over again to master it.

That really resonates with me because having character is a sequence of how you act every day. It is very much a habit you can form. I think you need repetition with character, just as you needed repetition with parachuting and with all that goes along with becoming a pilot. But those reps need to be done properly. It's an aspect of functional character, which manifests in persistence and work ethic, as we mentioned, and a willingness to listen to others. Were there any habits you fell into at an early age that helped you with parachute training and then your career after that?

When I think about it like that I'd have to tell you that growing up on the farm helped me become a better pilot—even plowing a field, because I learned that you control a machine, it doesn't control you. Over time, and I mean hundreds of hours on a machine, you get to feel the machine. You can feel how hard the tractor's working by the sound of the muffler or the feel of the engine's RPMs. You can feel steering. You can feel yaw. You can get a feel of a bulldozer if you spend enough hours driving one. When you first get in an airplane, it's exciting. You think, *Wow, now I get another dimension.* My whole philosophy in flying is that you don't get in as a pilot and strap in; rather, you get in and strap the entire aircraft to your body and make it an extension of your mind.

It becomes a part of you.

I know how it may sound to people who haven't flown high-performance aircraft, but you wear an airplane. Now, this was unusually tough with the Space Shuttle. It took me until my third mission, when I was finally a commander, to get my game face on and feel everything.

And the only way to get that feel is through intense repetition. You need to log the hours. It's the 10,000-hour-rule.*

Right. That feeling you get over time instills confidence. Because I was confident in my flying ability it made me a more confident flight leader. Then you up the ante. The next challenge is putting somebody on my wing—now I'm responsible not just for my airplane but I've got two guys in an airplane on my wing. You can kill all of them if you're doubting your abilities—so you can't. I wasn't the greatest athlete and I wasn't the greatest pilot, but when I was leading I had the attitude that I was. It's a mindset. It's not being cocky or overconfident. It's a state of mind.

I call it "confident arrogance," because as a fighter pilot you get to a point where you don't have to talk to anyone about how good of a pilot you are. You're confident in your abilities and your flying speaks for itself. I make that same comparison to the Cowboys in the early '90s. We'd walk on the field, we had confidence in ourselves and we had a definite vibe that we put out. There were games where we'd step on the field and I could see that the other team was already defeated. They might as well have not shown up.

Mindset is so vital—it can't be overlooked. That's another one where people forget it's actually two concepts together. Mind. Set. It's setting your mind toward a goal and locking it in.

When did you lock in the goal of going to space?

It was an evolution. When I was a kid I had a scrapbook of all the NASA missions. I kept track of Mercury, Gemini, Apollo, all of them. I'd cut the guys' pictures out of articles I'd find and read everything in Life magazine about them. At the time, it never struck me that I'd want to do that, or could do it. Even when I was at the Air Force Academy I was average academically so I didn't think it was a possibility. I graduated in the middle of my class and I was happy just to go off to be a fighter pilot. Then in 1976 or 1977, NASA put out the notice that they were looking for military pilots to apply to be Shuttle pilots. I was a 1st lieutenant as a 24- or 25-year-old, and when I looked at the job notice it said they wanted 1,000 hours in flight. I realized I was already at three or four hundred, so I applied in case they wanted me. They didn't. Two years later I applied again. No dice. Then I applied again the following year and didn't make it.

By then I was a captain in the Air Force. When I inquired about why I wasn't being accepted they told me that they really wanted test pilots for the job. Once I learned that, I applied for test pilot school and it took me three attempts to get in. When I graduated from test pilot school, NASA picked me up right away.

That is incredible persistence—three rejections from NASA then two rejections from the test pilot school. Talk about owning your vector in a huge way. You were knocked down five times and never took your eyes off your goal.

Becoming an astronaut became my goal. But I didn't have just one goal. Every time I changed jobs I would re-plot my map of the future. I had a piece of paper where I wrote down all possible promotions I could get from every job. This allowed me to visualize my career. At the top of the page I had jobs that I might be able to get fifteen years down the road. These were my long-term goals, like becoming a general, a wing commander, a Thunderbird pilot and also, yes, an astronaut.

What that allowed me to do was go about my career with a simple strategy. What job do I need to get where I want to go? After zigging and zagging on my sheet for a while, I finally made it to NASA in 1985.

What is the timeline from joining NASA to actually piloting the Space Shuttle?

The progression as a pilot in the shuttle program is you fly two missions before you get to be the Commander. Of course you have to perform in that role to move on, and fortunately I did. On my third mission I got to command the Shuttle, and it's a whole different game at that point, because legally it's like being the captain of a boat. I'm the captain of a ship in space and I am ultimately responsible for the ship and the crew.

Those are some pretty high stakes.

Yes. And this is where timing is important. You talk about stakes. I joined NASA six months before the Challenger accident, and I actually helped fly that crew down for launch. I had never seen a launch before and I thought I'd fly them in and hang out down there to watch the Shuttle take off. We all got to Kennedy [Space Center] safely, but the weather was getting cold so I went back to Houston thinking they weren't going to launch the next day. I was back at the office when the accident happened.

That's incredible. You flew the crew of the Challenger to their launch.

I did.

How do you move on from that? Did you think about leaving NASA?

Actually, right after the accident a former commander of mine, who had been my mentor, called me up and offered me a job as his director of operations at a base in Japan. He wanted me to fly F-16s and lead other fighter pilots, which I would have loved doing. He went on to become a four-star general. I knew I could trust him and I knew he was looking out for my career, but I turned him down.

Why?

The truth is that I really wanted to go to space and I was afraid that if I went back to the Air Force I would never get back to flying in space. I struggled with that decision, but I knew what I wanted to do.

Did you ever second-guess yourself?

No. I'm the kind of guy that once I make a decision, I stick to it. NASA had already invested a year in training me.

That's very much in line with one of the things Roger Staubach talked about: Your word matters. Sticking to commitments, regardless of what other offers come along, matters. Those are both very important aspects of having character. And when you add in the pressure of piloting a shuttle after a national tragedy, the pressure must have really cranked up.

Speaking of that, one of the jobs they gave me after the Challenger accident was to be the project officer for getting the shuttle from the west coast to the east coast. Remember, after we lost the Challenger there were only three of these national assets available. Now here I was, only a few years with NASA, and I'm responsible for getting a $4 billion vehicle from California to Florida and we had all these flying stipulations to worry about. We could only fly in daylight. We can't fly through clouds. We couldn't go above about 15,000 feet because there was no power on the avionics and the temperature change would cause condensation. Staying in the warm air meant we were flying low, which meant that the 747 was sucking gas so we couldn't fly coast to coast. We always tried to stop in San Antonio because it's exactly halfway, but having to land and take off twice for a one-way trip doubled the odds of something going wrong—and something always went wrong. Each one of those trips was an opportunity to extinguish my career.

And yet, as you've demonstrated your whole career, you persevered. I'm not sure if you look at it this way, but it seems like in your life you have managed to succeed in the wake of a tragedy several times over. From losing your cousins to losing

the Challenger crew, you picked yourself up and moved forward each time.

I didn't think about it like that as I was living it. But I never forgot what it felt like when my cousins died. Throughout my time in the Academy and thereafter, I continued to feel like I was doing things in my life for them; that I was living for them. That's why I kept pushing to reach my goals. I felt like I had to honor them.

So what would you say to a young man or woman reading this book who may have had similar experiences to you? Maybe they lost a loved one or a teammate. Maybe they are coming from humble beginnings and are in a situation where nobody in their family got an education beyond high school. What would you tell them about what they can achieve in life regardless of where they're starting out?

The first thing I would say is that they should never sell themselves short. If I'd have sold myself short I wouldn't have even gone to college. Nobody else in my family had, so it wouldn't have been a big deal to them. But for me, I would have never gotten off the farm. I think young people need to remember that this is the United States of America. You can do whatever you dream to do. And don't dream small. Dream big. Once you commit to a goal and start working toward it, you're going to get help from sources that you're not even aware of yet.

That speaks right to the idea of character being an ongoing thing. Once you start making positive decisions on the proper vector, more and more positive things are likely to happen. You have to put yourself on the right path and surround yourself with the right people. Then you have to capitalize on those relationships.

That's true. You can't get caught up in your achievements once you start having success. I learned early on not to brag and boast. I think a large part of having character is being humble. That will drive respect more than anything.

Absolutely. Being humble is tremendously important, and as someone who has spent more than 1,000 hours piloting the Space Shuttle, you'd have the right to be one of the cockiest pilots out there, but you're not at all. That's a huge testament to your character.

Thank you.

Thank you for your time. It's been an honor.

* The 10,000-hour rule is based on the Malcolm Gladwell book, *Outliers,* which posits that it takes roughly 10,000 hours of practice to display mastery in a field

Chapter 3

Virginia Prodan

"In the morning my children would come down for school and see me at the computer, and they'd say, 'Mom! You're still at the computer? You didn't move. You didn't sleep. You worked all night!' I just told them I was doing what needed to be done to achieve my goals."

I first met Virginia Prodan when I served on the board that gave her son Emanuel the nomination to attend the Air Force Academy. I didn't know much about her prior to that, but her son told their story, and then I met Virginia and she inspired me.

Here is a woman who grew up in Communist Romania; who became a political prisoner in her own home; who was interrogated, followed by secret service and ultimately threatened with death, simply for her belief in her faith.

Through international political pressure—and specific pressure from President Ronald Reagan—Virginia was exiled from Romania to the United States after years of house arrest. When she arrived, she had two children with one on the way. She had no money and she didn't speak the language.

What she was able to accomplish in her first five years in the United States and in the subsequent years of her life has been nothing short of jaw-dropping.

She has displayed a level of both moral and functional character that should make anyone facing a seemingly impossible task think twice, because Virginia's story proves that with hard work, perseverance and faith, anything can be accomplished.

Chad Hennings: So readers can have a frame of reference for your story and what you've been able to accomplish in your life, can you please explain a little bit of your childhood in Communist-controlled Romania?

Virginia Prodan: The way I remember it, my parents were always obedient outside of the house when it came to doing what was right and wrong in the eyes of the government, but then I'd hear them talk about what they really believe when they were inside of the house. I often thought to myself, *I don't want to grow up and live this kind of life. I want to speak the truth inside and outside of the house. This is not how I want to live.*

But I didn't judge them. They wanted us to have food, a house and have our parents at home. If they had spoken freely they would be in jail, but even knowing that, I thought the price was just too much. To have to live a double life and never be able to speak the truth was not what I wanted. Seeing them obey every day changed my life.

Approximately how old were you when you started understanding these things?

I want to say I was maybe six or eight years old. Another thing I remember that really shaped my life was that when we'd have family visit, I noticed that people always surrounded the lawyers and asked them questions. To me, as a child, they looked like they had the answers. I thought to myself, *I don't want to be like my parents, but maybe the only way to live is to be a lawyer and to know the truth and to speak up.*

Elaborate a little bit, if you would, on the idea of speaking the truth.

I grew up in a Communist country—Romania, under one of the cruelest dictators, Ceausescu, and his regime—where people were not allowed to go to church or believe in God. I went to law school in Romania and graduated at the top of my class because I was in love with the law and I looked at books as a way to gain knowledge and speak the truth—what was on my mind, not just what the government would let us say. I graduated from law school and practiced a few years of law, but I didn't find the truth and I was ready to give up.

Then what happened?

On one of the days when I was ready to give up, a client came to my office and he was very different from anybody else I'd met with. He had peace and joy and I was so mad and upset and I told him I wanted to have what he had in his life. He invited my family and me to church and I heard the gospel. I went from being a person finding the truth in law books to a person finding truth in the church. Well, shortly after that Christians came to me asking if I could defend them, and that's when I realized I was the only Christian lawyer. As soon as the government became aware of what I was doing they put me under house arrest, surveillance, regular interrogations, and all kinds of things. This lasted for several years.

The idea of your own government stalking you and questioning you for what should be a basic human right is such a foreign experience for Americans. Can you explain what it's like?

Before house arrest, I was followed by the secret police and my colleagues knew it, and many of them turned their backs on me because they were afraid the secret police would follow them. They would walk by me and look into my eyes and say, "I admire what you're doing, but I can't say it out loud. Please keep walking."

I remember one specific family I was close with. The wife was a lawyer and the husband was a prosecutor. Our kids used to play together and have slumber parties, and then when I became a Christian they started to find reasons to not let them play anymore. Eventually the husband became one of the people who interrogated me. He used to scream at me, "You are a lawyer! You're supposed to defend the dictator, our leader, not the religious criminals!" He became a stranger to me.

Wow. A friend ended up interrogating you for the government. You were able to see what people were truly made of, to really see their true character shine through.

Yes. I was able to see a spectrum of people and their character, for both the good and the bad, sometimes in the same person. In particular, I saw this on the night a man came to kill me in my office. This was after I was under surveillance in Romania but before I got house arrest. It was at the end of the day in my office and my secretary came in and said that a man had just arrived and he wanted me to take his case. She said that she had to leave and that he was a big man, so I was going to be alone with him if we were going to meet. I was thinking that he was a client and in need of help so I said that I would be fine.

When the man walked into my office, the only way to describe him is that he was huge, like a football player. I was eighty-two pounds at the time. He walked in, shut the door, and pointed to the chair in front of my desk. "Sit down," he said, very strongly.

I was thinking, *Why is this client ordering me around?* Then he said, "I don't have a case. I am here to kill you."

Then he pulled out his gun. I became paralyzed by fear. I looked at the pictures of my girls on my desk and thought, *I'm too young to die.* I was thinking that everybody warned me against taking these cases and being outspoken. I should have known this was going to happen, as it had happened to so many others. As this man stood before me, I heard the Lord say, "Tell him about me."

I heard this voice in my head and I remember thinking, *Lord, before I die you want me to tell the man who's going to kill me about you?*

You have to know that in Romania, because we didn't have any Bibles out in the open for risk of being caught, we had to memorize all of the verses by heart. So I just started reciting them. As I started talking he put his gun down and listened to what I was saying, and I could see him soften. I just kept talking, because I thought that the second I stopped I was going to die.

I was so scared, and in the middle of a verse I got a mental block and I froze. I couldn't talk. And I thought, *This is it.*

He paused for a moment and then said, "I will see you in church. I am not going to shake your hand, but I am like you." Then he walked out. I watched a man go from the darkness to the light.

He just walked out?

Yes. He just left.

That is an incredible story. It must have shaken you to your core.

It was horrible, but I survived.

After you were interrogated and had your life threatened, you were put on what you thought was permanent house arrest. How did you end up in the United States?

While I was under house arrest, our government was negotiating with the American government and President Reagan to get Most Favored Nation Status. Since I was in my house I was cut off from almost all outside contact, so I didn't know any of this was going on. Part of the deal for Ceausescu's regime to receive the MFNS was to respect human rights, including religious rights. As I was defending those human rights, part of the deal, unknown to me at that time, was that in order for Ceausescu to continue to receive MFNS he would not kill us but let me and my family leave the country.

One night my phone rang, which was very surprising because it had been cut off for so long I didn't know it still worked. I answered and someone said, "You have to come pick up your passport and leave Romania." I said, "I never applied for a passport." If you applied for a passport you were saying you wanted to leave Romania and that you don't like the country so they would put you in jail. That's why I had never applied.

The man on the phone said, "The government has decided that you have to leave or we will kill you. You choose." Then the American Embassy called and said that we should go to their building to fill out forms for our transfer to America. That's how it happened.

And to me, this is where you took your functional character to a whole other level. You moved to America, without knowing a word of English, with no money, with two children and one on the way. Somehow, four years later, you graduated law school and passed the bar in English. I'd love it if you could walk us through how you made the seemingly impossible possible.

Well, first, let me say that I did not have it in my mind that I would move here and follow history. By that I mean that generally when immigrants come to America, they start working low-level jobs to support themselves so that their children can have the opportunity to attend school and move up in the world. That was not for me. I wanted the best for my children but I was a professional in Romania and I was going to be a professional in the United States.

Even though I grew up in a Communist country, I had responsibilities every day and I had to plan. I was working from the minute I was walking. It was always, "Do your chores. Do your job. If you have any extra time, then you can play." So I knew no other way than to do work quickly. While I didn't know English when I moved here, I did know five other languages. Still, no English at all. It was very frustrating. I was a lawyer in Romania, and here in America I couldn't even read the street signs. I couldn't ask questions. I couldn't help my children with homework as they learned English very quickly. It was putting me in a depression.

I can imagine. How did you overcome the language barrier so quickly?

I was invited to several churches that were teaching English as a second language, but those were too slow for me, so I began surrounding myself with it. I put stickers all over my apartment with the words for the items and the pronunciations on them.

Like 'refrigerator' and 'cabinet' and 'wall'?

Exactly, yes. I also started watching the public access television channels and children's shows, like "Sesame Street." It was like learning as a kid all over again. I would get frustrated and yell at the TV sometimes to "please speak Romanian!" It was difficult but not impossible, and I knew I had no choice. I wanted to go to law school in America.

Again, perseverance. Work ethic. These are all such powerful traits of functional character.

That was all I knew. A funny side note is that I did learn English and I did pass the bar back then. Now my daughter, who went to

Vanderbilt and then Harvard, is also a lawyer. She went to a good

college and took LSAT preparation courses and she got a great score.

We were talking about it and it occurred to me that I passed the test

as well without any of that.

How did you find the time to study with three kids and a job?

What were your days like?

I had three kids to drop off at three different schools in the morning.

I never got a ticket, but I would be a liar if I said I never sped.

You do what you've got to do.

When I wasn't driving them to school or to their school activities, or

working as a research assistant for my [Southern Methodist

University] law school professors, I was studying. Also, during my

SMU Dedman School of Law years I was elected class president and

as the SMU Senator. My children saw me working at all hours, but

also taking care of them or being politically involved. Surely, working hard and long hours is the essence of my life. They would wake up early in the morning or late at night and see me on the computer. Sometimes in the morning my children would come down for school and see me at the computer, and they'd say, "Mom! You're still at the computer? You didn't move. You didn't sleep." I just told them I was doing what needed to be done to achieve my goals."

When my children were in college or working toward their own tests, they would call me sometimes and say, "You know, I have a test that I think is impossible to study for and I don't have time, but when I close my eyes, I remember coming downstairs and seeing you on the computer all night and I think, *if mom was able to do it, I can too.*"

Surely, as I was rebuilding my life I never imagined how much my hard work, determination and care for my kids influenced them. Just to give you a recent example, my son Emanuel, now a captain and rescue pilot in the U.S. Air Force, visited me in Dallas for a few days. He noticed that my laptop was getting older, so he bought me a new MacBook Air computer. I was overwhelmed and thanked him. But

Emanuel's response was, "I love you, Mom. You blessed my life in more ways than I can say; I hope to be a blessing back." This reminded me of the influence of my hard work and legacy.

That must be tremendously gratifying. You know, one of the aspects of character that several people have talked about deals with being a role model; essentially, influencing others to improve their character by displaying yours. You obviously walked the walk when it came to work ethic and your kids saw that and responded.

When my daughter first said something like that to me I was thinking, *Lord, I can die now. I did something for them!*

That's a phenomenal legacy.

Working that hard was all I knew.

Did you ever doubt yourself?

Sometimes things felt impossible. When I was accepted to law school at SMU, I showed up and I remember looking around and thinking, *Oh my gosh, these people are excellent in English. They're young. How in the world am I going to make it?* I was so afraid of not making it that I studied hard and finished in the top 25 percent of the class. Looking back on how I did it, I have no clue. I know sometimes, even for Christians, they may say I talk too much about God, but I can't take all the credit.

I want to ask you a little bit about your experience as an immigrant. As we talk about role models, I think some immigrants who come to America can be very positive role models because they bring a perspective that isn't skewed to our contemporary culture. As for you, coming from a Communist regime with a dictator, the idea of the freedom many take for granted has a whole new meaning, correct?

I think you're right. I received a pamphlet from the government when I first moved here that was so wonderful . It said America is the country where you can flourish. America wants you to be successful. We will support you, but we don't want you to be on welfare. We will not enable you. I think that's something that's missing today.

How was the culture different as you began to assimilate to the American lifestyle?

American people are honest, hardworking people, and generally ready to help others. I was encouraged by the "can do" attitude and so many smiling faces around me. In communist Romania, defeat, suspicion and jealousy were the norm and Christians were the only ones smiling.

When I got here I immediately understood that if you work hard, you can succeed. And I really believed that the people I was meeting along the way, the people who were watching me, were really happy for me. They wanted me to be successful. They wanted me to prove

that you can succeed in America no matter where you came from.

It was that palpable for you?

With every success, I felt like people were cheering me on. Everyone

was so positive. My son Emmanuel was born here and his

perspective was obviously going to be different than mine. He grew

up thinking that every house has a refrigerator and whenever you

open it there is milk and fresh food. A while ago I wanted to teach my

children about the value of freedom and I had the perfect

opportunity.

While I was living here in America, I became able as a resident to

vote in Romania's first free election. I didn't have any money to fly to

Romania, so I borrowed a van from a friend and drove all of us from

Dallas to Washington, D.C. to vote. I wanted my children to see how

important expressing your freedom is. I wanted them to pay their

respects to the concept of being able to vote. We dressed in traditional Romanian costume and we drove all the way there and voted.

That is such a valuable lesson. It goes back to what so many others in Forces of Character have said. Act with character to influence others. Do as I do.

That is true. Someone in the local media did a story on my trip, and after we had returned home I got a call from a friend who said, "If you drove across the country to vote, I should at least cross the street to vote."

The power of action. Tremendous.

Later on, when my children were older and I was able to vote here in the United States, I would purposely wait to vote until the end of the day on election days. I would pick them all up from school and I would say, "I have to go vote and you are all coming with me." They would whine and complain and say, "Nobody else is taking their kids to vote!"

But I told them it was a privilege and an honor to vote and I wanted to show them that. They didn't agree with me at the time, but if you talk to them now, in their twenties and thirties, they tell me they are thankful I took them.

Actions speak louder than words. You are a true woman of action.

You can teach through action. A short time after we moved here, one of my children had a problem with school, and how I handled it, they said, made an everlasting impression. My daughter, when she didn't speak English well, asked someone to help her understand how to use the combination on her locker in school. She thought the boy was being helpful, but there are good people and bad people everywhere. In this case, the next day, my daughter used the locker and when she went to get her lunch it was stolen. Then it happened the following day too.

My daughter came home so upset and yelling and asking me to go to the principal. I told her I would go, but only if she tried something for me for a week first. I said, "I am going to prepare a lunch for you and a lunch for the person who is stealing your lunch. We will put both lunches in the locker for one week, and if the person doesn't stop I'll go talk to the principal." My daughter said, "No, no, no… These kids have plenty of money, they don't need the food." But I made her try it my way, and after a few days the person was too embarrassed to take the lunch anymore and he stopped.

You took a tough moment and turned it into a lesson.

Sometimes we go through hard times because God is giving us an opportunity to teach something.

That's true.

I've learned that every person you meet gives you a chance to learn things from them. You either learn things that you want to do or things that you don't. I learned early in my life, because I was punished for everything, that it's much easier to learn from other people's mistakes.

That's great advice. What is the number one takeaway you'd pass along from your lifetime of learning from others?

Be a cheerful person. Learn what's nice about people and focus on that. When you are a cheerful and positive person, you are happy. People love to be with cheerful people.

Life is a legacy. Our lives and actions will influence our kids and others long beyond our departure. Working hard, being cheerful and having a winning attitude really make a difference.

Amen. We've touched on so many topics here, and the willingness to listen to others and to learn from others' mistakes is a unique angle on character. And you've displayed so many other traits in your journey. Personal responsibility. Accountability. Work ethic. It has been an honor to listen to your story. Thank you for sharing.

Chapter 4

U.S. Supreme Court Justice Clarence Thomas

"I've been at these jobs in various levels of government since 1981, and

what you learn is that it's not always that hard to make a decision....

The hard part is having the courage to say what you have decided."

I first became cognizant of Justice Thomas during his nomination hearings in 1991. At the time I was deployed in Turkey for Operation Provide Comfort I and II, where we'd fly to northern Iraq to help the Kurds and provide a presence after the first Gulf War.

It was such a pivotal time for the United States and my fellow fighter pilots and I were engrossed in the proceedings. We'd climb back into our room after the missions in the Middle East, well after midnight, and watch the Armed Forces Radio and Television Service. I'll never forget the night of the vote. We were all sitting there as it came down to the wire. One for. One against. One for. One against. It went on like that for some time, until finally, Justice Thomas was confirmed. When he got the nomination we all went nuts.

Several years later I finally got to meet him face-to-face when he spoke at a Dallas Cowboys chapel service prior to a game against the Redskins in Washington, D.C.

As he shared his personal story with us, I found myself becoming more and more impressed with the man and his journey. His ancestors were slaves. His father abandoned his family when Justice Thomas was two years old. His mother barely made any money, and when their house burned down they became homeless. Out of desperation, he and his brother moved in with their grandfather on a farm in Savannah, Georgia. Justice Thomas was seven years old at the time, and he finally had a father figure to look up to, his grandfather—a man that Justice Thomas has repeatedly said was the greatest man he has ever known.

From that humble start, Justice Thomas became an honors student in high school while working practically full time on his grandfather's farm, went to college and, as we all know, ascended to the highest court in the land, the Supreme Court.

While I listened to his story prior to that Cowboys game, I was thinking about how much we had in common in regards to growing up on a farm and all the life lessons learned there. The way he uses the agricultural analogies of life to find significance and substance in day-to-day tasks is truly genuine.

And what is most impressive to me, as you'll read in our conversation, is that while he occupies one of the most important, most visible positions in our entire government, he relies on the all-American character traits he developed on the farm as guiding principles for his decisions.

Needless to say, I introduced myself after his pre-game talk and I am proud to say we have remained in touch ever since.

How old were you when you first became aware of the concept of character?

Just from a personal standpoint—and remember, I grew up quite a bit ahead of you—the idea of character and right and wrong permeated society. It was every place you went. It was in the movies, when you watched Superman, when you watched cartoons, et cetera. I grew up watching Gene Autry on black-and-white television and he had a Cowboy Code for kids that said things like, "a cowboy always tells the truth."

When you hear that as a child you think, *my goodness, if Gene Autry says a cowboy always tells the truth then I should tell the truth.* His code also said things like, "a cowboy is clean" and "a cowboy is a patriot." You looked up to him, and when he said things like "don't be lazy" or "a cowboy must be a good worker" you tried to live up to that. You realized that you were always supposed to be a good guy. If you wanted to be a tough guy like Gene Autry or Hopalong Cassidy, you had to be honest, you had to be righteous, you had to be kind, you had to be good, you had to be clean, you had to be patriotic.

Were those ideals present in the community you grew up in as well?

It was all around you. Every place you went. You always addressed people with a handle on the name: Miss Smith, Mr. Jones. I grew up in a neighborhood where people were the working poor. You saw people who got up and did the right thing despite the odds being against them. There was segregation. Many people had no education. My neighbors were making $3 to $4 a day, if they had a good job. My mother made $10 a week, yet they all got up every day and went to work. They got on the bus, then they came home and they worked some more. This was when you didn't have air conditioning or microwaves, and most people I knew didn't even have a refrigerator; they had an ice box.

Anyway, the people around me were just good, decent, hard-working people who went to church on Sunday and who would share anything with you. Where I grew up people didn't lock doors to their homes. People left the keys to the car in the ignition or under the floor mat, or on the visor, you know? Growing up I never had a key to the house. My grandmother was usually home, but even if she wasn't the back door was unlocked. My neighbors' back door was unlocked. We were not a locked-up society. There was this sense that all around us people were supposed to be good.

Juxtapose that with today when many homes have an alarm system and every modern car has an alarm. It's interesting that you talk about us being in a locked-up society, because when it comes to character, so much of teaching it is walking the walk and talking the talk. Roger Staubach said that. Tom Henricks said it. It's difficult to point to people or even communities of high character when security systems and alarms inherently imply that if you don't have them someone will break in to steal your stuff and hurt you. It's a subtle but effective counterpoint to the idea that your neighbors are supposed to be good.

My neighbors would encourage you to be good. There was a trust. If, for example, my grandmother told me to go get a half-pound of bologna at the store and I didn't have the right amount of money, I could come back later and pay it. When people dealt with you, they expected honesty.

That goes back to the idea that if people want to be Forces of Character, their word has to mean something. Everyone I have interviewed has stressed that point. In order to have character, you must honor your commitments, act in accordance with your integrity and do as you say you're going to do.

It was considered the highest form of commitment, person to person, if someone gave you his or her word. In fact, if you asked someone to put their signature on a piece of paper after they already gave you their word, that was an insult. They'd think, *I gave you my word, you don't need anything else.* That shows you the importance of honesty. It was all around us. Right and wrong. Being righteous. Being kind. Being good. Being honest. Just being courageous. Doing the right thing when other people aren't doing it, that sort of thing.

What role did your grandfather play in your personal understanding of character?

When we went to live with him in 1955, I was seven and my brother was five. He said, "Boys, I'm never going to tell you to do as I say. I'm going to tell you to do as I do." Our job, according to him, was to watch him and do as he did. My brother and I were both raised by him. My brother died at the age of 50, but we were very close, and some time before he passed I asked him, "Was our grandfather ever a hypocrite?" He said "no." My grandfather lived up to his word. We both truly believed he was the greatest man we've ever known.

That's a very powerful statement. What was he like?

For one, I guarantee that these people who make it their business to interfere with the way other people raise their kids today would not allow my grandfather to raise us the way he did. My grandfather would always say, "Don't let the sun catch you in bed." What that meant was that if we weren't at school, we were working. And we weren't just pitching in. We were accountable for our work and we were subjected to very immediate corporal punishment if we messed up. He taught us that you've got to pay attention, you've got to do the work right and you can't cut corners.

Those are all phenomenal lessons.

I'll give you a great example. My grandfather would give me five gallons of gas and I would get on the old Ford tractor and he'd say, "Boy, go plow that field and make sure the rows are straight." So I'd go back there, and I'm plowing away and I'd look back and the rows would be crooked. I was a kid, but it literally became part of my life that I had to go back and re-plow those rows. Your first row has to be straight because then you set your wheel of the tractor on that first groove on the first row. If you cut a few corners early on, very quickly the field wouldn't line up and the last rows looked like hell. And who was going to be upset? My grandfather.

I totally believe that life is a series of building blocks. Character too. Your story hits home for me on so many levels. If you don't take your initial steps right, you may never achieve what you

want to later in life because those steps in the wrong direction have consequences. Just like that field. If your first row is crooked and you don't correct it, your last row will be even worse. This holds true whether you're studying for a test, learning a playbook—pretty much anything in life.

This is what I live by and it shows up in other places away from the farm. I left home at sixteen and went to seminary school, which was a boarding school. I was going to be a priest. We had to take Latin, so I had three years of Latin in high school. The courses were pretty aggressive and pretty brutal back then because it was one of the things that would separate the chaff from the wheat, intellectually and academically. One of the hard and fast rules of our class was that we were never to use what they called a pony or trot—that would be certain kinds of assistance in translating English to Latin or Latin to English, such as a translated version of the assignment.

So, for example, you could use an English to Latin or Latin to English dictionary, but you couldn't use a pony or trot. When you were doing your homework, you couldn't use a pony or a trot. Now, what did that teach us? By doing the work the hard way and doing it the right way, you learned more Latin. You learned Latin better because you skipped no steps.

That applies to almost everything in life and sports.

If you're weight training, you don't lift 100 pounds when you're supposed to be lifting 200. You don't do ten repetitions of a weight when you're supposed to be doing fifteen. Ultimately, you may be cheating and getting through the exercise, but in the end you're cheating yourself. It was the same principle with Latin.

It's definitely important for young men and women to learn the consequences of taking shortcuts, but I think the only way to truly learn that is to get bitten in the butt by trying to do something the easy way.

That reminds me of something I told my wife a while ago when I was thinking about my childhood. I turned to her and said, "I have no idea why I'm alive." Why did I think that? I spent much of my youth cutting down trees, and you and I both know that if you make a mistake with a tree, you're dead. I spent so much time cutting limbs off of trees, bush hogging them, or pulling them through the woods with the back of the tractor, et cetera. If you do these things wrong and that thing spins on you and gets hung up, you're done!

Think of the lessons you learn if you're dealing with stuff that could really hurt you. That if you perform a task wrong, the consequences are immediate and disastrous. What does it teach you? It teaches you how to do things right. It teaches you how to do it honestly, it teaches you how to not cut corners.

I named this book Forces of Character because I'm talking about character from the vantage point of physics. Force equals mass times acceleration. What this means is that character, whether good or bad, is a force. Mass, in this case, is the potential energy you have; acceleration is the idea that character is kinetic, meaning people build momentum by continuing to make high-character choices in their lives. You just gave a great example about character as related to work ethic, but I've always been

curious to ask you about how character is involved in your decisions as a Supreme Court Justice?

I've been at these jobs in various levels of government since 1981, and what you learn is that it's not always that hard to make a decision. The decision has its own analytical challenges, but you work through it. The hard part is having the courage to say what you have decided. That's the hard part, to say what you really think. To be honest. To tell the truth. In this city, whether it's political correctness or prevailing popular notions, there's always going to be pushback when you tell the truth.

You have to have the courage of your convictions.

Years ago, I was writing an opinion and the conclusion after. While we're doing that, we go back and forth with the clerks and we talk about all aspects of the opinion and we try to get it right. When we'd finally gotten it right, one of my clerks looked at me and said, "You're going to get killed if you say that." I looked at him and I said, "Is it the right answer?" He said, "Yes." I replied, "Then so we die."

I said that because what else do you do? Do you give the wrong answer because of fear? No. Does it mean you want to get beat up? No, you don't want to get beat up. But do you want to be able to look at yourself in the mirror? Yes. You take an oath to God to do this job right. In the end, you want the ability to find the answer, and you want the character to be able to stand up for it.

How difficult is it to become a clerk for a Supreme Court Justice?

There are thirty-nine clerks up here. That's it for the entire nation. Out of the hundreds of federal judges and all the law schools across the country, fewer than forty have a chance. So we're dealing with the crème de la crème de la crème in terms of ability.

What character traits do you look for when building your staff?

I look for intellectual honesty, and high levels of discipline and aptitude. I want to know how they work for other people or if they have ego issues. These are things I'm sorting for. I'm not a babysitter and I don't have time for drama in my chambers.

For example, my clerks and I meet every morning at 6:30. I didn't have to tell a single one of them to show up. This is the time they chose to meet. Why? Because I am here at 6:30 a.m. and we've got to get rocking and rolling.

That's when the work ethic kicks in. And I want to go back to what you said about character in the earlier part of your question. We do look for character at a very, very, very high level. When I start with new clerks, I tell them that they are going to see how decisions are made and that they're going to see a lot of things. But what I promise them is that when they leave this job with me, they will have clean hands, clean hearts and clear consciences. They will have to keep no dark secrets. They will only have to keep confidence, and those are entirely different things.

That's a lot of responsibility you're putting on yourself.

Well, it reminds me of a great line from Winston Churchill. Have you read much about Churchill?

I have. An incredible individual.

When Winston Churchill became prime minister of England, he had a great line. I don't know whether it's apocryphal or not, but I'm a big Churchill fan, and he said, "It was as though my entire life was but mere preparation for this moment." In my view, it's real simple; you shouldn't do jobs you're not ready for. This is my twenty-fourth term, so I've been up here now almost a quarter of a century.

As they say here in Texas, this ain't your first rodeo.

No. Do you follow rodeos at all?

Yes, I do.

This is slightly off topic, but have you ever seen any of the film on [the bull] Bodacious? I'd like to be like Bodacious, you know? If you notice, after Bodacious knocked one of these guys out, it turned and looked at the audience and just basically said, "I really kicked his butt." Then he walks out. He doesn't run out. See what I'm saying? My view is, you do your job. People do too much whining in society. Do your job.

It reminds me of a personal adage that I use as well. When people come across a situation they aren't sure how to handle, they should think, *What would John Wayne do?* And you know the answer. He'd cowboy up.

When I was new at this, back when I was chairman of the EEOC, people were beating the hell out of me in the media. It was very unpleasant. I was young at the time and hadn't gotten used to this sort of stuff so I asked my grandfather, "What should I do? These people are beating me up." He said, "Boy, you got to stand up for what you believe in." That's everything.

That's awesome. I want to be respectful of your time so we can wrap it up. I appreciate your honesty and transparency so much. This has been truly inspiring.

I admire what you're doing. I think it's really important. I think character is everything. And I'll be honest with you, I'm probably more idealistic today than I've ever been in my life and I believe that I have to give all credit to the good people in my life. There's no reason why I would have made it to adulthood if it weren't for the good people who influenced my life in this world.

Amen to that. Thank you.

Thank you.

Chapter 5

Bob Sweeney

"...Are you comfortable being where you are and doing what you're doing for the rest of your life? If the answer is no, it's time to get to work."

By doing some quick math, I can estimate that roughly 2,000 individuals are no longer homeless because of Bob Sweeney. He is a man who has dedicated his life to positively impacting other people, and I have been drawn to him since the first time we met at an awards ceremony honoring people for their volunteer and fundraising work.

I read up on Bob after our initial introduction and was amazed by the results he and his staff at Dallas Life have been getting in terms of converting homeless people to self-sustaining individuals capable of providing for themselves in the long term. The numbers are staggering, with Dallas Life achieving a success rate twenty-five times higher than the average national homeless shelter. Not twenty-five percent higher—twenty-five *times* higher.

Bob Sweeney is the executive director of Dallas Life, and the program he developed is the reason for such astounding results with this difficult and controversial social issue. He is a rare breed, and as you'll read in the following interview, he is on the front lines of our nation's struggle with the homeless. But by taking a tough-love approach that holds individuals accountable for their actions, he is winning the battle by putting one homeless person back on their feet at a time.

Whenever I sit down with Bob, a man of the highest character, I am motivated and inspired to live up to his example of selflessness and sacrifice. I am also captivated by his ability to connect with a wide range of people, from the indigent on the streets of Dallas to the insiders in Washington, D.C. I believe after you read this interview you'll feel the same way.

Chad Hennings: One of the missions of your organization is to work with homeless people and put them on a path to recovery and self-sufficient living. That's why I thought you'd be a fascinating interview on the subject of character—because you're on the cutting edge of building it. You take people who have lost almost everything and essentially reconstruct who they are, which leads me to my first question: How do you connect with people and affect change in them in the darkest moments of their lives, when they have no job, few possessions and no place to live?

Bob Sweeney: I think it's best to answer that with a real example. We have a couple who just graduated from the program. We'll call them Carl and Amy, to keep their privacy. They have seven children. One night last year they were evicted from their home and their belongings were literally dumped on the side of the road. With nowhere to go, they drove to their cousin's house and parked on the street. They had three of their seven kids sleeping in the backseat of their black pickup truck while they were taking turns showering in the cousin's house. In a brief period when Carl and Amy were in the house, the repo man came and repossessed their truck. It was dark out and he was in a hurry, and he pulled away and didn't realize the kids were in the backseat. Fortunately, he heard them crying and brought them home quickly. When he got back he told Carl and Amy he'd return in 72 hours for the truck.

That's devastating.

We hear these kinds of stories all the time. And this one gets worse. I'll never forget when Amy explained how they spent their nights once they lost the truck. She said, "We were sleeping in the park—or our kids were because we were huddled over them like a mama and papa bear watching their cubs. We all had one outfit, and we had to wash it at the gas station after a few days. Somebody's clothes would be hanging over the tree to dry. My kids weren't in school. We had nothing. Then we found Dallas Life."

Wow. There really aren't any words to comment on a scene like that. How do you even begin to build people up after such crushing events?

Before I answer that, let me first say that Carl and Amy currently have an apartment. They're showing character. They're getting deeper in their walk with God. They're spending more time praying with each other. They're realizing what parenting is supposed to be. Their kids are now enrolled in school and on the honor roll.

That's an incredible journey.

It is, and to get back to your question about how we build someone up, it all starts with accountability and expectation. When someone comes to us and agrees to work our program, we tell them how to do everything. We reinvent them. We tell somebody when to get up, when to go to bed, when to do everything. We tell them how their kids must act, when they have to be at school, all of it. Gradually, they'll take that structure on themselves. It takes time. This is the kind of structure that most people know by the time they're five or six years old. Stuff like remembering to brush your teeth, or to smile when somebody looks at you, or to hold the door for the person coming in behind you. Most people who come to our shelters and other shelters knew these things at one time, but whether it's oxygen deprivation to the brain, drug or alcohol consumption, or another cause, they just stopped realizing what was right.

So you're mapping out their lives, putting structure back into their day and holding them accountable. Accountability is such an important part of character. Both Roger Staubach and Tom Henricks, a man who went from driving a tractor to piloting the Space Shuttle, spoke about how important it is to hold yourself accountable when it comes to your character. If you can't meet your own standards, whose can you meet?

True. And when we start working with many of these homeless people, they don't have standards. So as we're gradually teaching them structure, they take on responsibility for the results of that structure. It ends when we've imparted the ability and responsibility to go get a job and support themselves and their families.

When it comes to lifting the lives and spirits of those around you, a form of moral character, how do you get the people you're trying to help to follow your lead and buy in?

I think one of the first things is to not lend any credence to their excuses. When the topic of homelessness comes up at meetings I attend locally and in Washington, D.C., I hear people say things like, "Look at the poor people. They can't help it that they're poor." I always reply with the same answer: Why are you taking all of the responsibility off of a person for their social status? We're all where we are because of where we were when something happened to us. You either learn from that event or it discourages you or crushes you.

How do those people giving the excuses respond?

Well, I usually give them the facts, which are these: Studies show that the average homeless shelter in America with a long-term recovery program of six months or greater is seeing a success rate of two or three percent. That means only two or three people out of 100 who leave the program never need shelter services again. That's dismal. With our program, we're seeing seventy-five to eighty people out of 100 never needing shelter services again.

That's a testament to the transformational nature of your program. To what do you attribute that high level of success?

Well, it's not because we came up with a new, innovative idea. It's common sense. Let's find out why somebody became homeless and go from there. People forget that most homeless people had a home at one point. If we don't find out why they lost that home, giving them another free home through the government is not the answer.

I think the question then becomes, how do you get someone to open up to you and trust you? This is important because trustworthiness, and the idea that your words matter, is a large component of character.

Gaining that trust begins by understanding who you're dealing with in whatever career or endeavor you're pursuing. In my world, that's homelessness. So what do we know? Well, the homeless used to be viewed as the guy who would have the stick and the bag hanging from it as he followed the rail line on the tracks. That is so far from what homelessness is now. They look like us now. Homeless people look like you and me, but they run out of money before they run out of month. That's what they are in the simplest terms.

Defining your audience in simple terms is a great way to get clarity on how to reach them. That's excellent.

And now that we've defined them simply, we can start to get a little more complex and break those people down into some categories. In this case, the five key causes of homelessness are: drugs, alcohol, money, relationship problems, and mental illness. So if I'm going to have any chance of these people listening to me I have to talk on their terms, which means if we're talking about getting involved with drugs or alcohol or having uncontrollable anger or any of the others, we're essentially talking about mistakes people have made. I have some of the most downtrodden, difficult, and honestly heinous people come into my office and you know what I find they respond to the most?

What's that?

It's not the rules or me laying down the law. The first thing they respond to is when I start telling them about all the screw-ups that I've made in my life. I start my conversations with many of these people by letting them know how I've screwed up. Immediately, I watch this barrier come down. Originally, they thought they were being summoned to my office to be forced to tell me everything that's wrong with them. Instead, I begin with what's wrong with me. They'll listen to that. I can see this look on their faces as I talk, which is one reason why I don't have a desk.

Explain that a little bit if you could. How does not having a desk affect your relationships with the homeless people you're working with?

I don't have a desk because if someone's brought to my office, they would naturally have to sit across the desk from me and they'd feel like they're in the principal's office. That's why I like the tables. In fact, I'll usually sit on the side and ask them to sit at the head of the table. Then they already feel like any air of superiority has been diffused and I'm not here to come down on them.

It's an expression of being humble, to show them that you're not above them in any way and you're here to help. I think that message could translate to a lot of bosses and coaches. It's easy to act like the big dog and to browbeat people into doing what you want. It's much harder to drop that veneer of power and be comfortable enough in your ability to know that people are going to listen when you talk.

It also symbolizes that you're on the same level. You're not here to show off your own position in life. The bottom line is everyone has had help in their life to get where they are.

That's true.

In our case with homeless people, I take the tack that if we really look at every person in front of us who's struggling as someone who just hasn't received any help yet, we can get our mind off of whatever rotten thing they did.

This is really powerful information. For anyone who wants to truly be a Force of Character they have to be able to positively influence other people. I'm hearing a step-by-step primer on how to do that from you and I'm grateful.

I appreciate you saying that. It reminds me that I jokingly tell our mentors that sometimes people don't sign up for mentoring because they think to be an instructor of anything spiritual you need to have the Bible memorized. I say you need four components for discipleship: You need a learner, you need a discipler, and you need coffee and you need donuts. If you have those four things you can talk to somebody about life, because just opening a conversation with, "So what would you like to talk about today?" is going to get you where you need to be.

Such a simple concept but it makes complete sense. As you were explaining that, it occurred to me that it's taken you a lifetime to master this skill, if you will, of being able to reach people and lift them up. Do you remember the first time that you displayed

this gift? Maybe a transformational moment where you began to understand what character is?

A story that comes to mind the most about character in general happened when I was in the fifth grade. There was a kid in our class named Keith and he had some sort of a disfigurement about him. He looked like he had a cowlick that covered his entire head and you just knew that all the other kids wanted to avoid him at all costs. I realized in just getting to know about him that he had a lot of pain from his past. I thought, *nobody's ever going to talk to this kid. Nobody's ever going to address this kid if he's just sitting here in this classroom the whole time.*

In the middle of that year, he moved into my neighborhood and he decided to have a party to welcome people over. I knew as soon as I got the invite that nobody from our school was going to go.

I took the issue to my mother, and I said this kid Keith is going to have a party at his house and I really think that nobody's going to go. I remember my mother went to the mantle and took this small China high-heeled shoe off of it and she said, "I guess this has been important to me long enough. It's supposed to help somebody else." She wrapped it up and gave it to me to take to Keith's house.

My brother drove me over to Keith's house and he pulled away while I was knocking on the door. Finally, Keith's mom opened the door and when I went in his father, his brother, his sister and his mom were sitting on the couch with him. Nobody else had come for the party.

The room was quiet, and here I was holding this box from my mom. It was awkward, but I handed the box to his mom and when she opened it she cried. I'll never forget it. That day I realized what character was. I learned that it's important how you treat people because you may be the only person that shows any care or concern for them. That was a very big day for me.

Wow. That's truly inspiring.

Yeah, and he probably owns a multi-million-dollar computer company or something now! (*laughing*) But I remember every moment of that day.

That is a phenomenal story. Other than your mother, were there any other individuals in your life who influenced your idea of character?

Brennan Manning has always influenced me, first through his writings and then when we met first about homelessness in 1999. He always drew me in because Brennan Manning was a Catholic priest who left the priesthood and married a former nun. Talk about lives that had been completely transformed! What I appreciated the most about Manning, and what he shares with people, is that one day he realized he needed a major change and he did it.

You have to have the conviction of your beliefs.

That's his whole thing. Whether it's a religious conviction or a personal belief, if you're trying to project an idea or way of life onto people while you're questioning it yourself, you really need to reevaluate things. That thought process was of great influence on me.

He would be a great example of transformational character, the idea that we're not perfect individuals. We all make mistakes or go down the wrong path, either through our actions, lying to others or lying to ourselves. The important thing is whether or not you course correct and get your decisions moving in a positive direction. At Dallas Life, you see individuals who are down and out, and yet you've helped them turn their lives around. What's the first step you take when it comes to transforming an individual's habits and character?

A lot of the residents we deal with in homelessness, whether it was in Michigan or here, have burned bridges throughout their lives. They've done things like stolen Grandma's purse for a dime bag of crack cocaine. Then when they enroll in our program, they immediately want to go to Grandma and say that they're getting better. Sometimes Grandma or whoever will never listen to their recovery. They'll say, "You stole my purse. Then you stole my VCR.

You're always strung out on drugs." It takes a lot for Grandma to believe this person has changed. When a resident gets upset, I remind them of this very important fact: You're never here for somebody else. If you've walked through these front doors to prove something to somebody, you're here for the wrong reason. You're always here because of what God's doing with you.

I think that will really speak to some of the young men and women reading this book. You can't become a Force of Character because someone else wants you to. You have to do it for yourself. It takes commitment. It takes perseverance. And above all it takes a desire to change. In your experience, how does that change happen?

For us, in the beginning of a program when a resident first starts, which we call Phase I, they often come in with a long list of what they think they need. I'll start by asking them this question very simply. I'll say, "What do you need?" In Phase I, so many of them answer like this: "I need the job, the car, the apartment, the check or the woman to take me back."

None of those are the truth. What they need is to find out why their root cause of homelessness has stopped them in their life.

Again, back to basics.

Yes. Then they get to Phase II and they'll take their classes on men's issues, women's issues and the psychology of addiction, and over two months' time they realize why they kept going back to that drug, why they kept stealing the VCR. Then, I'll say to them, "Now, why do you think you're here?" And they'll say, "I'm here for me." And I say, "You're almost there."

When they reach Phase III and they're looking for work and they have a mentor, I'll say to them, "Now why do you think you're here?" Then they'll say, "I'm here because God has chosen to get closer to me." And then I'll say, "Now you got it."

At that point, they're ready to begin entering the world again. I want to ask you about this stage of the process. You're getting people from a variety of different backgrounds who are destitute. How do you teach them or show them those traits that

will help them beyond the Dallas Life program? How do you teach things like perseverance, hard work, courage…the cornerstones of moral character?

I don't think you can help anyone until you listen to their entire story—because everybody's got one.

That reminds me of what one of my old coaches always says: In order to be successful, you have to coach the man.

That applies here too. I don't think there's ever a one-size-fits-all solution because everybody's journey is different. Whether you're on the road to recovery or the road to excellence, it's got to be an individualized road. Every homeless person who comes in here looking for help will have a tailor-made recovery program for them.

If we're talking about a young person who is the captain of a team or a coach running a team or even just a young person looking to become a leader, what is the mindset they need to connect with someone on that personal level?

One thing that is essential is you need to look at every person you want to help and you must realize that it could be you given different circumstances.

You're talking about empathy.

In a manner of speaking. For instance, there was a woman who came to stay at the shelter here and she said, "I know I can't stay." I asked, "Why is that?" She said, "Because I know you do a background check on everybody." I said, "I do." She said, "I did time for murder." I said, "Tell me what happened." She said, "My husband beat me for years. One night, he came home in a drunken stupor and he raised his hand to me. I grabbed the lamp and I hit him over the head and he died on the living room floor. I did all of my time in the penitentiary and I'm out now."

What she did not know was that due to various connections we have, I was actually able to get all the way down to the nitty gritty of her records in prison, and it's exactly the way she described it. I brought her back into the office and I said, "I just want to tell you that I did look over things and the only conclusion I could draw was that you were protecting your life in self-defense, and as a result of that I don't think you're a threat to anybody here, so you can stay. You'll probably be the first former convicted murderer that I'll allow to stay, but you're of no threat to anybody.

She looked at me with this incredible acceptance because she knew that I knew she told the truth. I didn't second-guess her or automatically believe she was lying. I thought about what I would do in her shoes in that exact situation. I think any of us in a position of authority have to do that.

It's interesting that you bring up the idea of authority. In the athletic arena, coaches, captains and team leaders are in a position of authority and their entire job is to get everyone on board, working toward one goal: winning. In that position you need empathy, but you also need to provide answers. How do you balance the idea of getting on the same level as someone while also imparting wisdom?

I think the empathy part is how you connect with someone you want to influence. You need to connect to the man before, as you said, you can truly coach the man. After that, you do need to have the answers. In order to convey them you need confidence. I've been running my program for seventeen years and I know what works. When I have residents who come here and say, "I can't read. How am I supposed to do the packet?" I say, "Well, there are answers to everything. Everything this side of hell can be fixed."

What we do is we'll put somebody with you who can help you learn to read. We have phonetics class. We have things we can take them to, to get their reading comprehension up to the seventh-grade level, which is a big deal. With a seventh-grade reading level, you can fill out a job application and get a driver's license. Ultimately, if someone is willing to work at it, we can fix almost anything.

Teaching someone to read is a tangible activity. You can measure the results and track progress. One of the challenges with teaching character is that it's a lifelong goal. It's not something that can be tracked from week to week. Rather, it's

the sum of a lifetime of decisions. Do you have any thoughts from your experience on trying to impart character versus teaching a skill?

Trying to impart character to someone takes time. The most important thing is that the people you're trying to reach need to see you living out real character. They need to see you accept them when they fail in an area of character. They need to hear about the times you stumbled and how you got back on track. They need to hear about your decision-making process when you were faced with a dilemma. They need to have a reason to be better and they need to see that behaving with character leads to a better life. I jokingly tell the residents, "We don't have a single class here at Dallas Life on self-esteem. Oprah would not be happy. What we have are classes on self-worth, which is far more important."

I appreciate the way you make the distinction between esteem and worth. Building on that, if you can convince someone of their own self worth, you can start painting a picture of what success looks like in their minds. For the young men and women

reading this who are beginning their own journey of character and discovering their own self worth, are there any thoughts you have about how to help them lock in a trajectory of success?

In our case, sometimes the best thing to do is try to talk to an individual about the consequences of not doing our program. If someone is homeless or has a mental illness that needs treating, we'll talk to them about the consequences of doing nothing. We'll ask, "How do you picture yourself down the road if you don't accept this help?" This is especially true of the suicidal people that we come across.

How so?

Well, what I normally say to somebody who tells me that they want to die has nothing to do with the act of suicide. I don't focus on them. I ask them to think about the person who will find them. I ask them to think about years down the road, how that person will deal with the flashbacks and memories of finding another human being dead. From that, I springboard into the conversation about what their lives will be like if they never take any steps to advance their life. I'll ask, "Are you comfortable being where you are and doing what you're doing for the rest of your life?" If the answer is no, it's time to get to work.

Amen to that. I think everyone reading this book has the mindset that it's time to get to work. Time to own their vector. Time to expand their capacity. Time to become a force of character like you, Bob Sweeney. Thank you so much for sitting down with me today.

My pleasure. Thank you for your interest and your friendship.

Chapter 6

Dr. Edith Eva Eger

"The biggest concentration camp is in your own mind, and I can show you that the key to get out is in your pocket."

Dr. Edith Eva Eger is an 87-year-old Jewish woman of diminutive stature. She may also be the strongest person I know. I met her through a Navy chaplain friend and I've heard her speak on several occasions. Each time she commands the room. I've even heard from several military friends that she has captivated groups of Navy SEALs and other battle-hardened troops. In a room full of tough people, it doesn't surprise me that she was the toughest. Here's why.

When Edie Eger was sixteen years old she was rounded up by the Nazis, put on a cattle car and sent to Auschwitz, the infamous concentration camp. While there, she witnessed unspeakable horrors, lost her mother and father and friends to the gas chambers, endured torture, and found herself starved to the point where she weighed barely sixty pounds.

As the Allied forces closed in on Germany, Edie and her sister Magda were moved to several different camps, ending up in the Gunskirchen Larger camp. Despite Magda's best efforts, Edie was so emaciated she frequently passed out and became unconscious, leading her guards to toss her in a mass grave in the woods behind the camp.

Fortunately, after the camp was liberated, an American GI from the 71st infantry saw her hand move and pulled her from the pile of corpses. She had lost almost half of her bodyweight and had a broken back.

As you'll read in our interview, Edie made a full recovery, married, became a mother and built a career as a world-renowned psychologist. Her story is impossible to listen to without gaining a newfound respect for what the human mind can endure in the face of hell on earth—and what humans are capable of when they have the right mindset.

I am blessed to have maintained a friendship with Edie since I first heard her speak, and I could think of nobody better to offer their thoughts on the power of having the right mental attitude, regardless of the situation. She is the epitome of moral courage, character and toughness.

Chad Hennings: Edie, I can't thank you enough for taking the time to talk to me. Your story is so unique and so awe-inspiring, and I want to be respectful of how you choose to tell it and where you'd like to start.

Edie Eger: Well, if we would have spoken a couple of days ago, it would have been the anniversary of when I was in the cattle car going toward Auschwitz.

Wow.

I believe I arrived in Auschwitz on May 20, 1944. I was sixteen. We were told we were going to Hungary to work in the fields. I'd never heard of Auschwitz, but when we got there I realized I was part of the Final Solution of Eichmann.

I've heard you speak several times, and you've said your mother told you some powerful words before you were separated. Would you mind sharing those?

Before leaving the cattle car, my mom hugged me and she said to me, "We don't know what will happen. Just remember, no one can take away from you what you put in your own mind," and she pointed to her head, and that's exactly what happened. Everything was taken away from me, except my mind and my sister.

And those words helped you survive.

Yes. I was told in Auschwitz that the only way I would get out of there would be as a corpse and I had no power over what was going to happen next. They could have thrown me in the gas chamber at any moment. When we took showers, we didn't know whether water was going to come out or gas, but I knew that they could never murder my spirit.

I remembered then, when I was sixteen, what I was told when I was about six years old, which was that God built me in such a way that I would not be able to control my external circumstances but I can control the manner in which I choose to respond to them—and that I shouldn't allow any circumstances to murder my spirit and my attitude.

You endured day-to-day horrors while in Auschwitz, but you speak about a particularly chilling experience with Dr. Mengele, who was known as the Angel of Death. Mengele liked to have inmates perform for him, and when he found out you were a ballerina, you had to dance while he discussed who he was going to send to the gas chambers. Can you share how you survived that experience?

When I was with Dr. Viktor Frankl*, it's very, very interesting that both of us used the same strategy. I told him that when I was dancing for Dr. Mengele I closed my eyes and pretended that the music was Tchaikovsky and I was dancing to "Romeo and Juliet." After I shared that with him, he said, "You know, when I was tortured, I too closed my eyes and imagined that I was giving a lecture at the Viennese lecture hall about the psychology of the concentration camp."

Many of the people I've interviewed for Forces of Character have talked about the importance of attitude, but it was often in regards to achieving a goal. You needed the right mental attitude to survive horrific conditions. Aside from your mother,

did anyone else make an impression on you in terms of teaching you about having the right mindset?

One of the very, very important people in my life was my ballet master. When I was a little girl, he told me that God made me in such a magnificent way, that all my ecstasy has to come from inside out, and that all my happiness and all my joy depends on the way I look at life, not from the outside in, but the inside out. I didn't know what he was talking about until everything was stripped away and everything was taken away from me, and I had nothing from the outside. That's when I found the power within me.

When you talk to people about overcoming the obstacles in their own lives, how do you talk about harnessing that power within? Can you teach people how to overcome things?

It's not about overcoming. I'll never overcome, but I can come to terms with it. I go through the very understanding of that with people.

You're talking about the power of the mind and dealing with stressful situations.

Yes, stress studies tell you that when anything stressful happens to us, we have two automatic responses: We either fight or flee. In Auschwitz, I could not fight. Many people did by attacking the guards, but they were shot right away. I could not flee, because if I would have touched the barbed wire guarding the camp I would have been electrocuted. I saw the blue bodies, so you see, you had to be very careful not to just run into that barbed wire because you felt so, so, so powerless. Many people did, and many people died before the Nazis even got to them. That's how strong our mind is.

What role does the mind play when you try to come to terms with what you've been through? Do you ever stop thinking about your experiences?

No. I have PTSD myself because I have flashbacks. Recently I parked in the back of a Costco and I faced a barbed-wire fence. Right away—right away—I was back there in Auschwitz, but thank God I don't

144

allow it to take over my life. It's fleeting, but I don't run from it either. I accept that. I think it's important. In the work I do as a psychologist, I guide people. They hold my hand and we go on a journey and we will visit the places they've been and live that experience; they relive it with me as if it would happen now, because you cannot heal what you don't feel.

In the grief work that you do in your practice, what is the end game for people? Does coming to terms with a dire situation or tragic event mean being able to take the next step?

It's to be able to revisit the places where you've been. I went back to Auschwitz, and that was very important for me to go back to that lion's den and reclaim my innocence and begin to forgive myself that I survived. Forgiveness has nothing to do with anybody else. It's about not allowing yourself to live with resentment and hatred.

Survivor's guilt can be very powerful and take many forms. While what you survived was on an entirely different level from the example I'm about to give, there are many people who come

from very dangerous neighborhoods and are able to attend college or even make millions in professional sports because of their athletic gifts. Many of them have lost friends to drugs or gang violence. What advice would you give to them about working through that guilt?

There is no forgiveness without rage. Don't cover things up. Don't medicate grief, but really go through the grief and the feelings and the healing.

I imagine it took you a long time on your own personal journey to do this.

Unfortunately, when I eventually came to America, I just wanted to be a young kid. I wanted to be like other people. I never told anyone I was in Auschwitz for many, many, many, many years. I had my secret.

How did it affect you?

In one instance, I didn't show up for my graduation because I had not only survivor's guilt but survivor's shame. I said to myself, *people survived who were prettier or smarter than I was.* I asked people to find the Nazi in themselves because I didn't even allow myself to pick up my cap and gown and stand. The biggest concentration camp is in your own mind, and I can show you that the key to get out is in your pocket.

Again, you're talking about mindset, and the reason I wanted people to read your story is to illustrate the power of the mind and the power of choice when it comes to character and everything else in life. In fact, what you've been able to accomplish in the years since you first came to America is amazing as well. Can you tell me a little bit about what it was like when you finally got to the United States several decades ago? It was your chance at a new life in a new world.

When I first came here I had my little girl who was two years old and I didn't speak a word of English. I didn't have six dollars to get on the boat, but the Red Cross gave it to me and I repaid it when I did my doctoral work at William Beaumont Army Medical Center. My husband ended up in a TB hospital and I became the breadwinner. I worked in a factory and I also went to school later and graduated with honors.

That is truly remarkable. And are you still a practicing psychologist?

Today I am known for my work with post-traumatic stress disorder, and I work with Vietnam veterans. I am very, very committed to the veterans and the homeless veterans and other military members. I'm a very grateful American citizen, because without the Normandy Invasion I wouldn't be here today, having three children, five grandchildren, and three great-grandsons. That's my best revenge to Hitler.

Amen to that.

I should say that I think revenge just gives you satisfaction and it's very temporary. Forgiveness gives you, truly, your freedom.

I was thinking that, in many ways, having character is as much about treating yourself properly as it is treating others. It's about having respect for your own well-being. In order to forgive, you have to make the conscious choice to forgive. Just like in order to survive, you have to make the conscious choice to have the right mindset. For readers of this book who are looking to improve their lives or climb out of a frustrating situation, what advice would you give them?

When I work with very successful people who grew up in a ghetto and places like that, there's one thing they all have in common. What they tell me is that they knew it was temporary, that they were going to get out of there. You see? Everything is temporary.

That takes us right back to mindset. It's all in how you look at things.

It is. When I talk to my patients, I tell them it's not about what happens to you, it's about how you handle what happens. Everything in life becomes an opportunity for an opportunity. And the aftermath doesn't have to be about recovery, but about discovery. I discovered my inner strength when everything was taken away from me. My parents died in a gas chamber and I'm here to tell you about it, so there you go.

If you could boil down all of your experiences to one piece of advice, what would it be?

For me, I enjoy every moment in life. I live in the present, that's what keeps me young. I don't care about my chronological age. I'm eighty-seven, and I go swing dancing every Sunday.

You do?

I have a wonderful gentleman who picks me up and takes me swing dancing and I live life to the fullest. It still pains me to throw out a piece of bread. I celebrate every moment of the gift of God and of having a second chance.

And if you had to define character, how would you define it?

Just to be kind and not inflict pain on other people. Those people are bullies. If you want to say something, ask yourself if it is kind, and if not, don't say it.

That's the golden rule. Do unto others. Thank you so much for your time.

Thank you, darling.

*Dr. Viktor Frankl was an Austrian neurologist and psychologist who survived the Holocaust and also wrote the best-selling book, *Man's Search for Meaning*. He also won dozens of international awards for his work in the fields of logotherapy and existential analysis.

Chapter 7

Carey Casey

"Your character will carry you much further than all of the gifts and talents and abilities you have."

Carey Casey serves on the White House Task Force on Fatherhood and Healthy Families, he's the CEO of the National Center for Fathering, and he's been featured everywhere from ESPN to *The New York Times* as an expert on fatherhood.

He also has spent time as team chaplain for the Dallas Cowboys, the Kansas City Chiefs and the 1988 United States Olympic team.

I've had the pleasure of hearing Carey speak many times and we've forged a friendship based on a wide variety of shared beliefs, including our faith, our volunteering efforts, our love of football, and our goals to positively impact our community and our society.

As one of the preeminent voices on fatherhood in the United States today, he is on the front lines of one of our nation's largest problems: how to instill character in a generation of young men who are growing up without a father figure in their home.

I greatly admire the way Carey goes about confronting this issue, as well as how he holds himself up, not as an example of someone living a perfect life, but as an example of someone dedicated to living a life

of integrity.

After this interview, you may admire him as well.

Chad Hennings: I know your father was a powerful figure in your life. Now that you're one of the nation's premier speakers on fatherhood, can you recall a transformational moment from your childhood when you learned about character from your own dad?

Carey Casey: When I was a little boy I heard someone call my dad the n-word, and how he handled it was a lesson in character. I was raised during segregation. I couldn't get ice cream at a certain store, couldn't ride in the front of the bus when I was real young. One day my dad walked into a gas station in our hometown and there were eight men sitting on bar stools. My dad said, "I need to get gas."

And this gentleman stood up over my dad. He was about 6'2" and my pop was about 5'9" or 5'10". I'll never forget it. I was probably six or seven years old. Anyway, this gentleman said, "We're not giving your n-word *blank*." And he used certain bad words. As a little boy, I sensed that there was going to be a confrontation, but my dad, with his intellect, his knowledge and his wisdom, he talked that man down. But this next part is the most important.

He turned to me first and said, "Son, evidently this man does not know my name." He was so calm. He didn't retaliate in a negative, demeaning way back to the gentleman. He then spoke to him quietly for a minute, and the next thing I know he went out and pumped the gas for my dad. When you look at the events in Ferguson and Baltimore, and things that are happening today, the reason my brother and I didn't have to retaliate when things happened in our own childhood was because we knew how to deal with authority by how daddy raised us. That was character.

The way you paint a picture of that story, it's almost the definition of what character is. Rising above a situation. Influencing others positively. Setting a strong example. What a powerful moment in your life.

My dad influenced me greatly. He even raises me more now from the grave than when he was here. There were things he said when I was a little kid that I'm just now getting, and I'm fifty-nine years old! I can't believe it. When I'm on a plane, when I'm getting ready to stand on the platform and speak or when I'm writing books, things he said hit me. I have three grown kids and an 18-year-old who just graduated high school. I have nine grandchildren. They literally know their great-granddad because of my life.

It's funny how that works. Are there any other transformational moments in character from childhood that stand out for you involving your dad? Maybe as you got a little older?

I do have one big moment that comes to mind and it involves another person of character, my high school football coach. One of the claims to fame in my life is that I was on the Virginia high school football team that lost to the Titans in the state championship game—[the Titans] from the *Remember the Titans* movie starring Denzel Washington. Well, the head coach of our team was white and he was the winningest coach in the state at the time.

Forces of Character

Anyway, a few months prior to that game when I was a sophomore, my coach got in my face about something. The next day I went into the cafeteria, and at that time blacks were on one side and whites were on the other. My black friends said, "Carey, quit the team. Don't play for that racist coach. Don't be an Uncle Tom."

When I got home I said to my dad, "I'm quitting the football team. I'm not playing for a racist coach." My dad got in my face and said, "Well, son, you're really talented, and if you don't play you won't have a team to play for. Your coach is not a racist. He's the winningest coach in the state of Virginia. He'll win with or without you."

Then he said, "You're not an Uncle Tom. You are a Casey, number one. You are a Christian, number two, and number three, that coach is checking out your character and your loyalty. You need the team more than the team needs you."

I'll never forget it. I went back my sophomore year and had a wonderful season, and that's how we ended up playing against the Titans. I still think about that conversation, and I tell people when I talk that they'll make a decision today, not tomorrow, that will dictate where their legacy will be thirty years from now.

I absolutely believe that. One of the concepts we're establishing in this book is the idea that character is kinetic. It's an ongoing process. As such, every decision we make affects our character either positively or negatively. Making poor choices can put you on what I like to call an improper vector, and that can lead you down the wrong path. It's important to start making smart, high-character decisions as soon as you can to establish a habit of strong character.

It is. And you know what? That coach my friends all said was a racist? My dad was the one right about him. When I was recruited out of high school—I'll never forget it—he put me behind his desk while the recruiters sat on the other side, and he sat in the corner listening to their pitch. He would sit in the corner and listen to what they were saying in order to get information to my parents and to see if I would even want to consider going to these other schools. He became one of my best friends. He just died two years ago. His name was Eddie Joyce.

Besides your father and Coach Joyce, were there any other major influences of character in your life?

Cowboys Coach Tom Landry was an influence on me as well. Coach Landry and my dad went to meet the Lord on the same day, February 12, 2000. Both of them were seventy-five years old, both of them were men of God, both of them were married to their brides for fifty years. I was the team chaplain, along with John Weber, for the Cowboys for some time when Coach Landry was there, and his integrity and character influenced me greatly.

With Coach Landry, you couldn't tell if we won or lost a game because of his character and how he would keep his poise and not lose his mind. That was the way my dad was, and it actually brings to mind another great teaching moment he had with me in high school.

I dropped a pass in a game before we played the Titans, and when I came off the field I was angry. I was kicking dirt on the sideline, and when I went back in the game I ran the wrong play. I was clearly flustered and I got benched.

That night after I got home, my dad took me under the maple tree in the backyard and said, "Son, you're going to have to learn how to deal with disappointment. It is not always going to go your way, and you're going to drop a pass sometimes. You're going to run a wrong play. The reason you're playing wide receiver and not running back is that your coach wants you on the field because he knows the next two years you're going to be his star running back if you play, but you don't see the bigger picture right now. You've got to learn how to deal with disappointment. He could not put you back in the game because it was all about you. You were so concerned because *you* dropped a pass." He said, "Son, that was one play out of the whole game. Y'all won the game. Y'all are going to the next level, but it's about you right now. You've got to learn how to deal with disappointment to mature and to make it in life."

What an incredible speech. I think that's something almost every parent should share with their child.

My dad had that kind of character. Tom Landry had that character as well, because even when it was tough, he still had his bride by his side. I remember it. This guy, we'd get off buses and planes, and Alicia Landry would be right there with him, and you couldn't tell whether we won or lost. He would still sign autographs for kids, he would still shake hands and be very gracious to people. He didn't go too high, didn't go too low. He didn't use a lot of words to show his character, but he didn't have to. He led by how he modeled.

Those are three strong men with strong personalities who all exemplified strong character. You're lucky to have had them in your life.

You know, I don't want to leave out my mother because one of the earliest times I can remember being taught right from wrong came from my mom. It happened when I stole some Bazooka bubble gum from the supermarket. I remember when we got in the car to leave I was passing around the Bazooka pack and opening up the cartoons that the gum was wrapped in. My mom turned around and asked us where we got the gum. My brother and sister said that I gave it to

162

them and I had to admit that I stole it. My mom drove us all the way back and she made me go in and pay the proprietor with money that she gave me. It embarrassed me like you couldn't believe.

If there's one theme from our family, it was that we stood for honesty and integrity and doing what's right, even when it wasn't popular and didn't feel good and was hard. Your character will carry you much further than all of the gifts and talents and abilities that you have.

Amen to that. And I should share with you that Roger Staubach and I had very similar lessons taught to us about right and wrong. And we were all affected in the same way because we all brought up these stories as transformational moments of character for us.

I think this is a good time to transition to the work you're doing now as a national speaker on fatherhood, because the commonality among your story and mine is that we had strong parents to guide us. A lot of the work you do is with kids who

don't have a father around or strong mother around to teach them character. What advice do you tell those kids who are looking for guidance?

More than anything, I would say find an older man in your life who can mentor you, who has been around the block. You can't navigate life by yourself. Men do not do well by themselves. You show me a guy, a gentleman, a man, or any father who does not have accountability, and I'd say they're destined to fall because we need that support. It's just like a team. You've got to have guys who will be able to get in your face. I would also say that they should gravitate toward men of integrity.

In your experience, what are some common traits of successful mentors, role models and fathers?

It's simple. You love, you coach, and you model. We've done lots of research here at the National Center for Fathering, and I talk about it in my book, *Championship Father: How to Win at Being a Dad*. Out of thousands of dads we researched, those were the traits of dads who loved their kids and were involved with their children.

In terms of character, I would think the idea of being a model of integrity for your children would hold the most water. When I interviewed Justice Thomas of the Supreme Court, he said his grandfather, who was his greatest character influence and raised him, told him as a boy to simply watch what he did and act accordingly.

That's in our research, in fact. Personally, my dad modeled for me. When I saw him get called the n-word, he showed me how to handle that kind of situation and it has stayed with me to this day. I'll give you a quick story illustrating my point.

A few years ago I went along with about twenty CEOs to play golf at the nice courses in Wisconsin. We go on a golf expedition every year. One day I was going to get my clubs and a gentleman got out of a nice, sleek automobile, and he comes over to me and says, "Sir, will you get my clubs for me?" He didn't know I was playing. The people at the golf course said, "No, this is Mr. Casey. He's the CEO of the National Center for Fathering and he's playing here." They were worried I was going to sue the golf course and get big money and be on the front of the newspaper.

Some people with me asked, "Why didn't you tell that man who you are? Why didn't you let him know what you've accomplished?"

I didn't have to because I saw my dad model for me how to handle those situations. I didn't need to belittle that man or prove to him who I was. My dad taught me that in the story I told you earlier. You have to know who you are—even when others don't.

The best life lessons last a lifetime.

They do. And in my work, especially with NFL players today, I see too many young men who don't have someone to teach those lessons. Case in point, I was in a movie last year called *Irreplaceable*. They were interviewing me at Arrowhead Stadium. At one point I gestured toward the tunnel the players run out of to get to the field and I said, "You see that tunnel right there? Fifty-three guys on each team will run out on game day, but you know, many of them would love to one time look up in the stands and see their dad sitting in one seat, looking down at them and giving them approval."

You had that, Chad, growing up in Iowa. I had that. But when guys do not get that they have what we call a father wound. They are searching for where they come from and who they are. Although they have a jersey with their name on the back, they make big money, they're identified with the NFL, they're identified with Air Force or North Carolina where I played, they are still searching for an identity. When a young boy or girl does not have a father in the home, they're more likely to be poor, drop out of school, be involved in crime—and girls are more likely to be pregnant as a teenager.

But just by a dad being there, those statistics flip-flop. Kids need authority. They need a father, grandfather, or father figure. When a kid has that, they will not only survive but they will thrive.

Now we're talking about being responsible and holding yourself accountable for your actions, which is a form of moral

character. Having a child is the ultimate responsibility, and from what you're saying, when fathers don't accept that role, the negative impacts on their children and society in general are devastating.

Yes. When I speak at sports chapels and I ask, "How many of you don't know your dad?" Boatloads of hands go up. I ask, "What's one word to describe your father?" They don't even know me sometimes, and they'll start saying, "Absent. Cheater. Loser. Coward." They're angry. They're angry in their hearts. That's why some of those guys lose their mind sometimes and choke their wives or girlfriends; they have this pent-up anger because they resent not being taught and being mentored by a man.

My dad taught me how to tie a tie. He taught me how to talk to my kids. How to dress for an interview. How to conduct myself. How to treat a woman. I'm el nerdo like my own dad sometimes. My kids, they'll say, "Dad, you pull your pants up too high and you wear lace-up shoes," and all this type of stuff, but that's the way my dad did it.

Here's a funny story. One of my sons is thirty-two now. He's married with a seven-year-old, a five-year-old, a three-year-old, and a one-year-old boy. Three girls and a boy. Do you know I watch him, and every time he comes over to the house his pants go up higher and higher? I'm not kidding! I am serious. When he wears a Polo, he buttons it up all the way just like I do, but I'm el nerdo. Like father, like son.

But as I was saying, if a son doesn't have a father, it's painful. Even if these young guys don't admit it, they want somebody they can look up to and share their heart with, and many times I'll look them in the eye and say, "Come here. If your dad left you when you were a kid, and you don't know where he is or who he is, or your dad treated you terrible and you only saw him one time, and he told you you were dumb, stupid, you're not going to amount to anything—if your dad could see what I see today, he would be so proud."

Too many times when these kids were growing up they were told they'd never amount to anything. The reason we're cursed in America today is the breakdown of the family—a dad gives that child character, which is what you are talking about with this book. The real character comes when a kid has a father, grandfather, or father figure. Do the research in the Dallas Morning News. Pick it up today and see where somebody's done something stupid, or some type of crime. They probably did not have an involved father. I'm talking suburban, I'm talking urban, I'm talking rural. If that dad is not involved in that child's life, they're not getting what God wants them to get. Some dads are rich, have boatloads of money, buy the kids cars, have a nice home, all this, but if they're not involved and engaged with that kid, that kid can do some crazy stuff.

The obvious question for me here is this: How do you replicate yourself and what you're doing out there to promote fatherhood and to help young people in need of a role model? How would you encourage other individuals to be that mentor?

Well, quite naturally, those three things I say: love, coach, and model. I can do that for my family. I'm the patriarch of my family. I'm not perfect. They see my best and my worst, but even with the toughest of situations I have to keep my poise. I have to be the head coach of

170

my family. In my book, *Championship Fathering*, I talk about it, and here's the deal: Love, coach, and be a model for your kid, but then pay attention to those kids right in your own neighborhood and sphere of influence who don't have a father, grandfather, or father figure. Those are the kids you can help.

When we moved into our nice suburban neighborhood seventeen years ago, there were three young boys living right next door to me. Their father left when the youngest was two. That being the case, I entered a relationship with them. And guess who they call Dad? They're white and I'm African-American and I've become their father figure. When they were growing up they'd put a note on my windshield if something happened in their lives and they needed guidance. The note would say, "Dad, can I talk to you about something today?" We've become that close.

If you want to affect change, start in your own neighborhood. There's really nothing like leading by example. Thank you for that excellent piece of advice and for all that you've shared. Any last words of wisdom?

The greatest thing I can do is be a man of God, a husband, and a father. The rest is icing on the cake. When you walk with integrity with God, and none of us are perfect in that, but when you do that, the results are going to come. My dad wasn't perfect, but I felt like I had the best.

Chapter 8

Jason Garrett

"When it comes to character, you have to somehow, someway, summon

the best version of yourself in everything you do."

Most people reading this book know Jason Garrett as the head coach of the Dallas Cowboys. But I have the pleasure of knowing him on a slightly more personal level: as a roommate.

Jason and I were basically rookies together and were roommates in our first away game in training camp. We played in the American Bowl in Japan our rookie year, and after that he went to the practice squad and became our third-string quarterback. We were teammates for a long time after that.

One of the things that has always impressed me about Jason is that he's such a quality human being. His father was an NFL scout and he was always around training camp. When you spend time with someone in the presence of their dad you really get to know who they are as people and where they came from. I can vouch for the fact that Jason has a strong lineage and I always knew he was headed for a successful coaching career.

What I admire about Jason, and why I wanted to talk to him for this book, is the road he took to playing in the NFL and the path he took to becoming an NFL head coach. He didn't attend a high-powered college program and didn't get drafted in the first round and become a starter in the NFL. He went to an Ivy League school and spent most of his NFL career as a backup. But despite not seeing much playing time and not coming from a traditional football school, Jason earned respect wherever he went by displaying a rock-solid work ethic, a dedication to his craft, and an uncanny ability to relate to players from all walks of life.

And now, as the Cowboys' head coach, he's entrusted with establishing a culture of winning and character with perhaps the most recognizable team in all of professional sports.

Chad Hennings: First I just want to say how great this is to be sitting here, in front of Tom Landry's desk, in the office he designed, talking to you as the Cowboys' head coach. I remember getting signed in here. Every great player and coach in this organization has been in this room. And having played with you and watched you develop as a coach, it's really gratifying to see your success.

Jason Garrett: Thank you. Some days I come in here when it's quiet and I realize I'm sitting behind Tom Landry's actual desk and I pause to take it in. It really is special.

So much of the history of the NFL was shaped in this room. And that brings me to my first question. As head coach of the Cowboys, the leader of America's team, we all know what your goals are in terms of wins and losses. But in terms of character and having a personal impact on your players, what do you try to achieve?

My job as the head coach of this team is to create an environment where everybody can be their best. In terms of our players, we try to give them structure, give them inspiration, give them instruction; whatever they need, that's what we'll do. Now, I certainly have to live up to that myself. It's a daily challenge but I think it's worth the challenge. When it comes to character, you have to somehow, someway, summon the best version of yourself in everything you do.

When I look back with regret on certain situations, it's usually because I wasn't able to do that. And that's not just with football; it's with relationships that you have, things you're aspiring to do, your family, everything.

Life lessons through football.

Yes. There are a lot of different definitions for mental toughness, but the one that we believe and we talk to the team about is the idea of being your best regardless of circumstance. What does that mean? It means there's never an excuse, or an explanation, or a valid reason for you to not dig deep inside to be your best. Whether we're talking about a response to adversity, a response to success, a family thing, a team thing, generosity, thoughtfulness, whatever it is. We should all aspire to be our best, and that's really the atmosphere we try to create here.

Our players hear me talk about being their best ten times a day. That's what this life's about. We're trying to live the best version of ourselves. What I mean by that is we all have different choices we make every day, and you can choose to be strong enough mentally, physically and emotionally to be what we're capable of being.

Mental toughness, focus, the commitment to being your best. These are all aspects of functional character that can take a lifetime to learn. Who has most influenced you when it comes to having these character traits?

I've been incredibly fortunate in my life to have been surrounded with some great people, but I'll start with my dad. He is an amazing guy. He's eighty-five years old, and when I think about his work ethic, his generosity and his passion it inspires me so much. We lived in a house where he would bound down the stairs or burst through the front door. There was so much energy and it was just so positive.

And reflecting back on it now, I realize it must not have been easy to do that every day. I have seven brothers and sisters. My dad was a football coach and my mom is a saint. All of the kids are about a year apart and we moved all over the place. I think there were so many kinds of built-in values that were part of our upbringing. With eight kids you had to be a good team member, but we didn't talk about it in terms of a team, we talked about it in terms of being a good brother or sister.

I also saw great leadership from my parents. My father had an incredible work ethic. He'd wake up early, come home late, and we could feel the passion for what he was doing. And my mom was just selfless, making sure everything was right all the time. All the lessons you learn growing up in an environment like that apply, and I think character is at the root of all of it.

Do any specific examples of that positive mindset and passion that your father had stand out to you from your childhood? Anything that has stuck with you to this day that you think about in your own life?

Oh yeah. I think about his attitude and perspective on things all the time. Whenever we had to move when we were kids, he would talk about it like it was going to be the greatest place ever. "We're moving to Texas. We're moving to Louisiana. Have you ever been to Cleveland, Ohio? That place is great!" You know? Boom. And there was so much energy to that.

These weren't simple moves. You're talking about a wife, eight kids, three dogs—I mean, these are significant things. We're all going to new schools, and just the perspective that my parents had on it, it was always like we were embracing an opportunity and the attitude they had about it was instilled in all of us. In hindsight, it was great. It was great to live in different places, to have to overcome different things and put yourself out there with a new group of people and not be afraid of those situations. Mental toughness is so important and that's what it taught us.

It sounds like your mom had to be pretty tough too.

Yes. My mom was the same way. She just had this amazing calm and poise about her. We didn't talk a lot about right and wrong; there weren't these big sit-down lessons, but it was just us watching how they lived and it was pretty amazing.

You know, it's funny that you told me your story about stealing the football card and how impactful that whole experience was for you. I have a similar story that I just thought about as we were talking about my mom. We lived on the corner of Ocean Avenue and Beach Road in Monmouth Beach, New Jersey. At the corner there was Lou's Mart. It was a three-minute walk down the street.

In the back of Lou's Mart there was a bunch of Bazooka Bubble Gum with the comics inside. It was all right there. I remember one time I reached up and grabbed the Bazookas and just walked home. I was five or six years old and I walked in chewing Bazooka and reading the comics and my mom asked, "Where'd you get that?"

I remember having that tearful "I took these" response and my mom made me go there and give it back. You think it's the absolute end of the world—you're crying about it, you're emotional about it—but it's the greatest life lesson a parent could ever share with their kids and you remember it the rest of your life. I think those kinds of things start defining what's right and wrong for you and it really becomes part of your DNA going forward.

Just so you know, I've interviewed Roger Staubach for this book as well, and even he stole something as a kid, so we're in good company!

Roger did?

Something about us Cowboys, I guess. (*laughing*)

I guess. (*laughing*)

I think the crucial thing to remember is that each of us had someone in our lives who cared enough to let us know we were veering into dangerous territory, even though we only stole small items and we were kids. To borrow a flying term, I like to say that we were put back on the proper vector. In our cases, it was a parent who helped us out. But in many cases, it's a coach or teacher or someone in the neighborhood. Were there any other strong influences of character in your life besides your mom or dad?

I've done talks on coaching and leadership and I always ask people, "Do you guys know who Eddie Reinhardt is? How about John Malone or Frankie O'Brien?" Nobody has any idea who they are so they all shake their heads 'no'. Then I say, "Those are my seventh- and eighth-grade coaches who had such a big impact on me."

I think as much as anything else, it comes back to work ethic. So much of it comes back to a standard of doing something; so much of it comes back to handling adversity. One of the great things about football is it's all about handling adversity and being strong through successes, being strong through harder times—whether it's responding to a play or a series or a game or an injury or all of those different things that happen to you throughout your career.

And, to this day, I think about some of my high school coaches like Cliff Foust and Fred Heinlen. A lot of what I share with our team, if I really traced it back, I learned from my high school coaches. It carries all the way through college and the NFL. Also, every one of the coaches who influenced me talked about coaching the person first as opposed to the football player. That's definitely an approach that we try to adopt here with the Cowboys. Develop the character of the person first, and that's going to reflect in the character of the player. That's a big part of our whole philosophy here and I think I trace it back to my parents and all the coaches I've had along the way.

You've had a slightly different path to the NFL as both a coach and a player because you played your college football at Princeton, an Ivy League school known more for academic excellence than as a football powerhouse. What did you learn

from your time there that you've taken with you in your coaching career?

I think I probably learned more about excellence there than any place else. There were really, really smart people all over campus who were interested in a wide range of things. I was certainly most interested in football, but I think I came to understand that there was a lot more going on in the world, and there were a lot of really impressive people who were interested in being excellent in what they do. You think about different departments in a university like that. Think about the innovations in the molecular biology lab or what they were doing in engineering.

What did you major in?

I was a history major focusing in recent American History. I did my senior thesis on the black power movement of the 1968 Olympics.

Really?

Yes. I wrote about a guy named Harry Edwards. He is a sociologist. I don't know if you've seen him, but he used to be on the 49ers' sideline and he organized boycotts at the college level in the '60s. What was happening was a lot of black athletes were having great impacts in college but they weren't being treated the same way as the white athletes. One of the great examples was this huge track meet at the New York Athletic Club. All the great black athletes at the college level, the amateurs, would participate and they're the ones who made it so famous, but they couldn't stay at the New York Athletic Club. Only the white guys could. So eventually they boycotted things at the college level, they boycotted stuff like that and that eventually influenced John Carlos and Tommie Smith.

That's amazing.

One of the other things that I thought was interesting about Princeton was The Honor Code, which I know you had at the Air Force Academy. Over the course of four years at Princeton, I think you understand the importance of taking advantage of this opportunity to learn for learning's sake because of that. I think that was real. It probably wasn't real for most of us initially because we're thinking about what grade we were getting and if we were keeping up, but at some point you realize that, wow, this is a great opportunity and you look around and think, *if I take full advantage of this, it could really be life-changing.* I certainly have taken that concept with me into my coaching career. I've said before that I think coaching is very process-driven. It's learning for learning's sake. It's doing things the right way and letting the results take care of themselves.

When I hear you say that coaching is process-driven, I instinctively think about the habits that establish those processes. When we talk about character, one of the concepts I've explored in these interviews is that character is kinetic; it's the sum of countless decisions throughout your life, and the only way to consistently make positive decisions is to make it a habit to do so. How do you work on instilling those processes and those positive habits in your players?

Simple. It's repetition. It's working with someone like Dez Bryant and making him run the route, run the route, run the route, run the route, run the route, over and over again. Then you talk to Dez and say, "You have a chance to be one of the all-time greats. You have a chance to be better than Michael Irvin. You have a chance to be someone who brings the championship back to Dallas."

We're drilling him but we're also instilling in him the idea of this opportunity that he has and where he can go and what the heights are for him. He can wear a gold jacket. He can be like one of these Hall of Famers. We're drilling them, but suddenly the desire to be great is coming from inside. They want to be part of something special.

That's a really great example and it sets up my next question perfectly. For a young guy like Dez, or anyone on the team or in your life who you want to influence like that, how do you get them to buy into doing all that hard work? I know Dez is motivated, but what about others?

Well, it starts with showing them examples of what we want. With Dez as a rookie, we said, "Dez, run the routes, you can be one of the greatest, watch [Cowboys Pro Bowl tight end] Jason Witten."

That speaks to the idea that we have to be great examples as coaches and also have the best players on our team be great examples. This raises everyone's game. I really think you need this approach. As coaches, as parents, as mentors, that's what we do. If it's your kids, you're saying, "Do your homework, do your homework, do your homework." If you want them to read more, you're saying, "Read a book, read a book, read a book, over and over." That's good, but you have to set the example. They need to see you reading books regularly as well. Suddenly, they're more likely to enjoy reading. I think those are the things that we're trying to do every day in developing the character of the people around us.

I couldn't agree more. Having character takes a day-in and day-out effort, and in order to truly have a transformational change in someone, it needs to be constantly guided. It can't just be a

one-off conversation. Eventually, that person has to own it and make it a part of their persona.

Absolutely. Because at some point, whoever it is, the kid's going to leave home. He's going to go to college. He's going to graduate from college. The player has to go on the field by himself. The player is going to have to work out for four weeks before training camp by himself. This idea that we're just going to beat it into them, that's part of it, but the other part of it is they've got to eventually get it themselves. They've got to "own it," as you said. They've got to work toward their own goals.

They've got to own it, amen. But even with the right examples on the field, and coaches saying the right things, you still have to personally get through to a player as the head coach. How do you impact some of the young players who have had a totally different background from you?

We believe that you need to develop relationships with players. We believe you need to have some kind of connection with them.

Sometimes with this idea of someone being a "player's coach," there's a perception that the coach is easy on the players. That's not the case at all. In our case, we strive to drive the players. We also want to develop a relationship with them, we want to connect with them, we want to be able to communicate with them.

I tell our players all the time that the coaches I hate to this day were the ones who used to pat me on the back all the time and say, "Boy, you're doing a great job." I'd throw a ball clear over a guy's head and that coach would say, "Boy, you're doing a great job."

The coaches I loved, the guys for whom I literally travel around the country and go to their kids' weddings, are the ones who just drove me and drove me and told me it's never good enough. "Can't you do that faster? Can't you get it out of your hand faster? You need to have more command. You need to take charge." Whatever those things were that I needed to get better at, they never were satisfied. Those are the guys I love to this day.

That's the kind of environment we're trying to create here. With a guy like Dez Bryant, to develop a relationship with him, that's important. Also, we hold him to a high standard. He knows that we never think it's good enough. He knows we're watching him, and that with each play he could've come out of that route faster, could've tucked the ball away more, he could've used the stiff arm, he could've been sharper out of that break. Whatever those things are, that's the relationship that we have. We're going to push you and drive you, and I do think that allows you to connect with them. It also helps them reach their personal goals while we reach our team goals.

As far as reaching your own goals, when did you know you had a real chance at becoming a professional athlete? Not too many quarterbacks make it to the NFL from the Ivy League.

Because we were around professional football with my dad, it's what I always wanted to do. Whether or not I truly believed that I could do it, deep down it's always what I wanted to do. I had such a passion for it, and working in football came very easily to me. I had such a desire to do it. My parents tell me stories where I used to drag a bag

192

of footballs down to the basement in our house in Cleveland in the dead of winter and throw a ball into a blanket for hours. I was fourteen years old. It was a part of me that way. I also had other contraptions set up in the house to help me throw. I used to throw into mattresses, and this was usually after my brothers caught a ton of balls for me.

I figured I'd work at it whenever I could and if I took each step one at a time, maybe I'd have a chance to play in the NFL. First you do well in high school, then you go to college and then you have a chance at the end of that. I certainly wanted to pursue it in every way I could.

I think that dialed-in, laser-like focus is necessary to make it and it's a sign of functional character. By that I mean resilience, work ethic, attitude, positive attitude, coachability, great determination, perseverance—those kinds of traits. Were you aware of that differentiator that you had in terms of desire at a young age?

Yes, no question. I would say that in all sports I played, I always worked very hard and cared a great deal about them. But there's no question that football for me was just so much more important. I had so much more passion for it. Not that I didn't love playing basketball or playing baseball—I played more baseball than anybody on the planet—but the football thing was something that came from within me. I wanted to play it more. I wanted to get better at it. I would say the degree to which I was committed was much higher with football.

Speaking as your former teammate, that commitment to the game was something that we could all see. It was why you had so much respect. Now that you're in this upper echelon of coaches in sports, are there any other coaches you've come across or received advice from who pushed their players the right way to build that connection?

I thought Jimmy Johnson was fantastic at it. He pushed us and I think he developed the right relationships. He created the right environment and he instilled confidence in everybody. I thought he was amazing.

Somebody else I've spoken to and spent some time with since I've been a coach and who's really had a big impact on me is Coach Mike Krzyzewski from Duke.

I went to visit him for three days once, and I went to Cameron Indoor during a regular Friday practice and it was the most amazing practice I'd ever seen, and I've been to hundreds and hundreds of practices. Every facet was amazing: how the coaches interacted with the players, interacted with the managers, how the drills were run, the serious nature of it, the intensity they had, the communication everybody had with each other, the seamlessness of the drills. I'm sitting there for half an hour and I'm like, *there it is. This is what it is. This is the secret of the whole deal.* It ran like a machine. The precision in everything they did was just off the charts.

He's such an impressive individual.

And here's another aspect of it. After practice we go to the meeting room and one of Coach K's best players, Kyle Singler, from a few years ago, was in a bit of a shooting slump. I watched Coach K talk to his staff for forty-five minutes about how he was going to engage Kyle to help him out of his slump. He discussed whether he should go see Kyle or have Kyle over to his house. They put together a video of Kyle looking strong and shooting well. He rehearsed the story he was going to tell Kyle about the first high school game he saw him play. This went on for forty-five minutes and he was asking his guys the whole time, "What do you think?"

I was in awe. This is the greatest coach there is, and the care that he spent talking to these guys about how to present himself to this player, who's one of his best players in a little bit of a shooting slump, was incredible. I thought to myself, *I just saw one of the best practices I've ever seen in my life, and then we come in here and we talk about this kid and how we're going to talk to him for literally forty-five minutes.* It's the greatest combination I've ever seen. It's IBM and it's mom and pop. It's relationships. The practice is hard, he drives these guys, but he has these relationships with these kids, with these coaches, with these managers that are just unbelievable. It's impossible not to want to do and be your best around them. To me, he has the great balance. He's done it in every way there is and he's certainly someone we aspire to be like as best we can in everything we do.

What an incredible story. Character at its finest. Thanks for sharing that. I want to be respectful of your time and your practice schedule, so let's end with that great anecdote. Thanks for taking the time, Jason.

Thank you, Chad.

Chapter 9

Gregg Popovich

"When I think about character I want to know about the fiber of an individual."

To me, San Antonio Spurs Head Coach Gregg Popovich represents the quintessential model of continued excellence. He's been at the helm of the Spurs for almost twenty years, and in that time he's won five NBA Championships and three Coach of the Year awards.

What's even more impressive, and what is most pertinent to this book, is that San Antonio has built a reputation as an organization known for its high character. In fact, if you do a Google search for the words "Spurs" and "character" you get more than three million hits.

In the current era of sports, where athletes are often jumping from team to team for the highest paycheck, Coach Popovich and his organization have created a climate in which their best player, Tim Duncan, and the other stars of the team, consistently take below-market value to stay there and continue the winning tradition.

On a personal level, I know Coach through the Air Force Academy, where we both attended. I'm excited to take this opportunity to get to the core of how he has led a high-character organization for nearly two decades, and what he looks for when it comes to adding talent.

Chad Hennings: When people talk about the San Antonio Spurs, they mention the five championships, they talk about you and Tim Duncan and David Robinson, and inevitably they talk about the high character of your team. How have you gone about building that reputation and infusing character into your organization?

Gregg Popovich: Sometimes when I hear people talk about character I think it's a little too general of a term. We've all seen a million books on it and everybody's got a different definition of what makes up character. People always say our teams have character and they know how to win, know how to lose, all sorts of those things. I try to be a little more specific in my definition, especially when it comes to the character of players we bring in.

Can you explain that process a little bit and get into the nitty gritty of your definition of character?

When I'm interviewing a kid to draft I'm looking for specific things. Over the course of sitting in the gym and talking, having lunch, watching him at free agent camp, this is what I'm after and not necessarily in this order.

Having a sense of humor is huge to me and to our staff because I think if people can't be self-deprecating or laugh at themselves or enjoy a funny situation, they have a hard time giving themselves to the group.

You look at a guy like Tim Duncan. He never changes his expression but he can hit you with some of the best wise-ass comments in the world. I can be in a huddle, laying into him about his rebounding, saying to him, "Are you gonna get a rebound tonight or what? You haven't done anything." Then on the way out of the huddle, he'll say, "Hey, Pop." I'll say, "Yeah." He'll say, "Thanks for the encouragement," and walk back on the court. He's being facetious, but nobody sees things like that. I think when a player has that ability and has respect it's a good thing.

It's funny you bring this up because nobody has mentioned the idea of having a sense of humor in terms of character, but you're right, it really is important. For levity, for relationships, for leadership, humor can be a very effective tool. And it's great that you use Tim Duncan as an example of that, because most people might not be aware that he's a funny guy. What are some other character traits you look for?

Being able to enjoy someone else's success is a huge thing. If I'm interviewing a young guy and he's saying things like, "I should have been picked All-American but they picked Johnny instead of me," or they say stuff like, "My coach should have played me more; he didn't really help me," I'm not taking that kid because he will be a problem one way or another. I know he will be a problem. At some point he'll start to think he's not playing enough minutes, or his parents are going to wonder why he's not playing, or his agent's going to call too much. I don't need that stuff. I've got more important things to do. I'll find somebody else, even if they have less ability, as long as they don't have that character trait.

That really is a good indicator. If someone is always blaming other people for their shortcomings, chances are they'll eventually blame you too. So much about having character is taking responsibility for your actions and putting yourself on the proper vector for success. What else do you look for?

Work ethic is obvious to all of us. We do that through our scouting. For potential draft picks, we go to high school practices and to college practices to see how a player reacts to coaches and teammates. The phrase that we use is seeing whether people have "gotten over themselves."

When there's a guy who talks about himself all day long, you start to get the sense that he doesn't listen real well. If you're interviewing him and before you ever get anything out of your mouth he's speaking, you know he hasn't really evaluated what you've said. For those people, we think, *Has this person gotten over himself?* If he has then he's going to accept parameters. He's going to accept the role; he's going to accept one night when he doesn't play much. I think it tells me a lot.

I like that. "Has this person gotten over themselves?" Such a simple question, but the answer speaks volumes. If they haven't, they can't give themselves to the team and won't put the work in.

Right. We also look at how someone reacts to their childhood. Some of these kids, as you know, had it pretty tough coming up. Once in a while somebody has had it easy, but for the most part a lot of guys have had some pretty hard knocks already. I like to hear situations where they had to raise a brother or sister, or where they had a one-parent family or a grandma or grandpa raised them and they still ended up doing pretty well academically in high school.

I like to see if they participated in some function in the community, or if they've overcome something or had a tough injury and came back. That sort of thing tells me what kind of character they have. I think all those things together tell me about their inner fiber. When I think about character I want to know about the fiber of an individual. I want to know what, exactly, they're made of; what's attached to their bones and their hearts and their brains. It's all those things that form their character to me.

It sounds like you're really searching for selfless individuals. Are there any things that you do in practice to reinforce those traits? Anything you've done during training camp? I heard you took your team on the ropes course at the Academy a while back. That must have been part of that philosophy.

A couple of years ago in the Finals we basically gave away a championship, long story short. Heading into the following season I wanted to do something different. I wasn't trying to be Mr. Tough, but I wanted to do something to build camaraderie and respect for each other. I wanted the guys to go through something difficult with their teammates.

One day at camp that year the busses picked up the team from Antler's Plaza downtown. They thought we were going to the gym for another practice, but we went down to Jacks Valley,* and when we pulled in the players were wondering, *What the hell?*

The bus parked and we started to get up, but I said to the coaches up front, "We're getting off." Then I told the players, "You guys stay seated for a bit." We got off the bus and sergeants came on and started raising holy hell. Just like when we were Doolies.**

The players' eyes sprung open and they started to ask questions, but the sergeants yelled back, "Are you talking to me?!" The guys were in shock. They didn't know whether to start laughing or to say, "Hey, Pop, what the hell are you doing?" There was silence on the bus except for the sergeants. They marched the team off of the bus, got them in line and put them in squadron formations. It was unbelievable.

The coaches and I were behind a tree just dying. We couldn't believe it. I didn't really know they were going to go that far, and it's a testament to the kind of guys we have. They were willing to listen and they'll do what you ask them to do.

All of a sudden the sergeant who was in charge said, "At ease, everybody relax." He started laughing and then the players looked at us. We started laughing and now they're having a ball. The sergeants issued them all a rifle and gave them a little talk, and they went in twos onto the obstacle course. We had guys on the ropes. We had Tony Parker falling in the water. Tim Duncan's going over every obstacle, and I was scared to death because I envisioned a reporter asking me, "When Timmy broke his back falling off the log, what were you thinking? How smart were you to do this?"

But that's him. He wanted to do it, and one of his legs doesn't even work. He still did it, every single deal. That was the greatest thing. When it was over, they said it was the most fun and the most interesting thing they had done in their careers. For me, the camaraderie of it, seeing each other in those circumstances, rooting and cheering for each other, it was worth a million dollars.

When your biggest stars like Tim Duncan buy into your system, it has such a trickle-down effect to the team. How can a guy on the bench not participate if the future Hall of Famer is giving his best?

Speaking to that, the other thing I'll do in practice on a regular basis when we run drills, is I'll purposely get on the big boys the most. Duncan, Parker, and Manu Ginóbili will catch more hell from me than anybody else out there. You know the obvious effect of that. If you do that and they respond in the right way, everyone else follows suit. The worst thing you can do is let it go when someone has been egregious in some sort of way. The young kids see that and you lose respect and the fiber of your team gets frayed a bit. I think it has to be that way. They have to be willing to set that example and take that hit so everybody else will fall in line. It's a big thing for us and that's how we do it.

Too often you see organizations treating a few people differently for whatever reason and it's a problem. I was on a few teams where some guys got away with murder and everyone knew it and it killed the team.

You always see that.

It's not rocket science, is it?

I go to bed every night and I don't worry about anybody on my team. I don't come to work in the morning and say, "Ah, jeez, I'm going to have to clean this mess up." It doesn't happen. Everybody else spends half their time cleaning up everything or trying to convince themselves that this guy and that guy get along and blah blah blah. When people ask me how I do it, I just think it's total logic. You don't have to be smart. I realize it's not easy but a lot of guys don't get it. When they have problems I say, "You did it to yourself." There are no problems if a team does the work ahead of time and uses character as a "true" component of selection.

When it comes to dealing with the kinds of players who may become a problem, those kids as you mentioned who may have come from tough backgrounds, do you ever try to impart life lessons or lessons on character through basketball?

Sure. I think it's really important because it's the right thing to do. We spend a good deal of time discussing politics, race, food and wine, international events, and other things just to impart the notion that a life of satisfaction cannot be based on sports alone.

We work with our players on things as small as how they talk to the media. Things as easy as saying, "I'm doing well" instead of "I'm doing good" when someone greets them. It seems like a little thing but it's important. My daughter still gets on me about that all the time when I say, "Oh, I'm good," and she says, "No, dad, you're well." It sounds better, like you really went to school and paid attention.

I think working on some guys' speech and how they react to the media really helps them have a more productive life. We do things on our team board like vocabulary and state capitals to see who gets them quickest before we start practice, just to get the guys thinking. Through those kinds of exercises you may find out that somebody's not included over and over.

When you finally figure out why—maybe a kid can't read very well—you get him in the room and you get him lessons. You have a little bit of a tough day because he's embarrassed as hell, but then the kid starts to learn how to read and feels pretty great about himself.

That kind of off-the-court stuff is so important.

I'll go to dinner with a guy and it'll be the first time he's ever eaten an oyster or the first time he's ever had a glass of wine. Whatever it might be, you're spending time away from the court.

Building those relationships is crucial, especially if you want to have an impact on someone's life. Several people I've interviewed for Forces of Character have brought up the importance of coaching the individual, meaning, you have to know a person before you can truly influence them and get them to buy into your team's goals.

I've been doing this a long time, and one of my biggest joys is when somebody comes back to town with their kids, or one of my players becomes one of my coaches, and you have that relationship that you've had for the last ten years, fifteen years. It might be only three years in some guys' cases, but the lessons they learned from you paid off—even if you traded them or you cut them. Years later they come back and say that you were right, that now they know what you were telling them.

I think all of that relationship building helps them want to play for you, for the program, for their teammates. Beyond that, from a totally selfish point of view, I think I get most of my satisfaction from that. Sure, winning the championship is great, but it fades quickly. It's always there and nobody can take it away. The satisfaction I get from Tony Parker bringing his child into the office, or some other player who came through the program and now I hired him as a coach and he's back. That's satisfying.

You can't just get your satisfaction out of teaching somebody how to shoot or how to box out on a rebound. That's not very important in the big picture of things. If you can have both I think you've got some satisfaction. It's one of the motivations. That's the selfish one I guess, but it's real.

Thank you for your honesty, Coach. I've always been curious to ask what you enjoy most about coaching, and now I know. I'm also curious about your individual experience with character. As the face of what is considered to be one of the best-run franchises in professional sports, what moments in your life

shaped your view of character? Does anything from your childhood standout in terms of transformational moments where you got your first taste of right and wrong?

Sure. I think most of us have those moments. I've got one. When you say right from wrong, it's a dichotomy: you learn the right way from doing the wrong thing. Another part of character is the first time you get knocked down and if or how you step back up. In large part this can be a measure of your character as your life proceeds, because everything is not going to go your way. You're going to get knocked back and you're going to have to step up. I have a moment that stands out in both of those arenas.

As for the right-from-wrong thing, I can still remember in high school we had a gymnasium and then a floor above it that went around. There were bleachers up there and on one end there were cemented baskets.

At lunchtime they'd put on the music and people actually danced in the gym after you went to the cafeteria. Well, one day, all of a sudden there's a fight up there and I'll never forget it. The guy in the fight wasn't a close friend or anything, but there was this little scuffle up there and I was a bystander. This kid got hit and banged his head on the cement floor and just laid there. Blood started coming out of his ear and some people ignored it, while other people stared.

The bell rang and I just went back to class. To this day I get a twitch that I should have done something. I should have either tried to stop the fight, or I should have stayed with the kid, or I should have gotten help. But I didn't do anything and I felt like a coward afterward. That was really the first time I saw something that I knew was definitely wrong and out of whack and I didn't perform well.

You know, that story is a great illustration of the power of choice and the ramifications our decisions, or indecisions, can have. At that moment, had you done something, you may have felt how good it was to help out and it still could have been a big moment for you. The fact that you held back and you regretted it may have had an equally large effect on you as well. I guess if you didn't regret it that would be telling too. What about the

other aspect of character you talked about regarding overcoming obstacles?

As far as personally getting knocked back, I'm from Indiana and basketball is king there. In the town I grew up in, East Chicago, Indiana, that's all you thought about. I got cut as a sophomore and didn't make the team. I'll never forget that feeling, that devastation at that age. All of my buddies were playing. After that, I'd be up there at those baskets incessantly, playing every chance I got. I ended up being captain of the team and the leading scorer as a senior. Coming back from that was the first time I really learned that you can take control of your life. You need to understand that life's not always going to go your way but you're responsible for participating in your own recovery.

That's great stuff. When you were experiencing that devastation and that frustration, was anybody around to help you push through it? Your parents, your coach—who were those individuals that had a big impact on you? Or were you internally

driven and motivated to spend that extra time to push through and make the team?

There was a JV coach, Mr. Vermilliou, who was also a chemistry teacher, and a baseball coach, Mr. Hutchison, also a math teacher, who were fantastic with me. They'd give me keys to the gym and I'd come at night. The next day they'd ask me how the workout went. Once in a while they'd stop by and give me some pointers on what to do conditioning-wise. I think those two teachers were more important to me than anybody else. I wasn't real close to my stepdad and my real dad was gone. Those guys were the ones I looked to.

Keeping with this line of questions, you went to the Air Force Academy, then active duty, then started your coaching career. Who are some of the men who helped you or mentored you along your trajectory?

As far as the Academy is concerned, Hank Egan was the most important guy to me. He's a Naval Academy grad and I think he's eight or nine years older than me. He was the JV coach. I was a wise-ass coming from Indiana playing ball. I wasn't recruited. I was one of the only guys who ever played basketball there and wasn't recruited.

As a sophomore I played JV ball, but the whole time I thought I should have been on the varsity, as we all think we're better than we really are. Hank Egan was my coach; John Clune was the head coach. Of course Coach Clune—Professor Clune, Colonel Clune—he's passed on, but he was a great inspiration. Hank was the day-to-day guy who worked with me. I tried to quit five or six times and he's the one who kept me in the Academy. He's the one who kicked me out of practice every two weeks for being a jerk and just rode my ass. I went to his house quite often. Afterward, when I came back to the Academy as a coach in the athletic department, I spent a lot of time at his house with him and his wife Judy, who fed me many times. He was probably the biggest influence while I was at the Academy.

As far as coaching, is there anybody out there who you've tried to pattern your style after or who you particularly learned from?

It seems odd, but I've tried not to pattern myself on anybody. For two reasons. I think technically, as coaches, we pick up things from everybody we played for, coached with, or played with. There might be certain things I could point to. With Coach Egan, I learned how to make practice plans and how to organize a good practice. Larry Brown was a great tactician. Coach [Don] Nelson was a great manipulator. As far as strategy, I think you pick up things from everybody. As far as your style, are you going to be a Bobby Knight type, or be laid back, or be considered a really classy guy like John Wooden, or be Mr. Personality like John Calipari, a great recruiter?

But in terms of actively trying to be like one of those guys, I've always felt that could be dangerous because, number one, players have great BS antennas. You have to be yourself above everything else. I know what's good and bad about me. For instance, I curse too much. Whenever players curse around me I'll say, "Jon, you don't have to do that, be better than me. You don't need to curse, you sound ignorant, you don't need to do it."

They'll look at me and stare like, "Wow, I'm playing for a crazy man. This guy's cursing all over the place and he's telling me not to." But it works because they know I'm being honest and I'm being earnest. I think that's the key. Your approach, your demeanor, the level of negativity or positivity, I think depends on the individual. I think if you pattern yourself you can get in trouble. When I see good in people, I'll tell them sometimes I wish I could be Johnny Wooden, but I just can't so get your ass in gear. That kind of thing.

I was doing some research about your career before this interview, and I was looking at some stats from your first head coaching job at Pomona-Pitzer. You struggled a bit out of the shoot that first season, but then you righted the ship. In terms of achieving goals and maintaining the positivity for you and your staff and players, how did you overcome that? And what lessons did you learn along the way?

That season wasn't a *bit* of a struggle. I was 2-22.

I was trying to be nice. (*laughing*)

It's a really academic school. It's a hell of a place, but when tryouts came around only twenty-five people showed up. Maybe three of them had played on their high school teams. It was a little strange. We went 2-22 and lost to CalTech, which hadn't won a game in I don't know how many decades. It was a real comeuppance. The only satisfaction was, instead of losing by twenty-five and thirty-five every game, we were losing by ten and five, but they were still losses. That was my first real awareness that you need good players to be successful. No matter what kind of coach you are, you might get the group to achieve at its highest level, but it still may not be a winning group.

My second year, out of fourteen or so varsity guys, eleven or twelve of them were freshmen because I recruited them. Then I became a better coach. Who could guess? I learned it's the players. That's the first time you learn that. You can bust your ass, but then you better have people who can play or you're not going to win at the highest level. It was a learning situation for me because I thought I was going to come in there and be God's gift to the world, and I got slapped pretty good.

That's a great lesson to learn. Great players translate to winning seasons, which lead to a culture of winning, which is what you have with the Spurs. What role does reinforcing winning habits play in all of that? I ask because one of the themes of this book is that character is kinetic, that it needs to be exercised and that people need to be proactive to maintain it. Is that how you see it?

Absolutely. I look at habits as very important in life. Good habits are just like working out: if you don't get the habit, it's hard to get it later in life. The more you do it the easier it is, the more it becomes part of your life. For me this comes from the Academy. Habits and doing the right thing—even though you're tired, you don't feel like it, you want to skip it.

I had the same experience at the Academy. My last question is simple: Is there one piece of advice regarding character or work

ethic, or any of the topics we've covered, that has been especially valuable to you over your career?

When I was at the Academy I took a course by an amazing man, Colonel Malham Wakin [now a retired Brigadier General]. He used to teach a class on the morality of war, which sounds like an oxymoron in one sense, but he would make sense of it. He would do it on a moral basis, on a religious basis, on a humanistic basis, on a practical basis. He wrote a paper called *The Taste of Lemons.* You can still get it and I keep it to this day. It's about the taste of a lemon; you don't like it but the more you do it you get used to it. If there's some activity or some job, or you have to apologize to someone, or whatever it might be, that's the taste of a lemon to you. It's not fun for you, but the more you experience the taste of a lemon the more you can do the right thing. That's what I've always kept in my mind.

That's outstanding. The Taste of Lemons. Thanks for your time, Coach.

Thank you.

*Jacks Valley is the training complex on the grounds of the United States Air Force Academy

**Doolies is a term used in the Air Force to refer to freshman cadets

Chapter 10

Troy Aikman

"Without integrity and without character, I just don't believe you can lead at all."

Troy Aikman can flat-out lead.

We won three Super Bowls together with the Dallas Cowboys, but more important, we pretty much came into the NFL together and I got to watch first-hand one of the great leaders in our game develop.

Troy was one of those guys who put his money where his mouth is when it came to work ethic and grinding it out in practice every single day. He worked just as hard when the Cowboys won two games his rookie year as he did after he won Super Bowl MVP.

He got knocked around and lost a lot of games his first couple years in Dallas and I think it really humbled him. Fortunately, he had so many high-character traits that both he and the Cowboys weren't going to stay down for long. He had extreme focus. He had perseverance. He had integrity. He could motivate people. He stayed positive and kept a team full of big personalities and future Hall of Famers in line.

I interviewed Troy because he exemplifies so many traits I've covered in this book. He led when things were tough and he led when things were great. In this interview we'll explore the people, moments and habits that made him the man he is today.

Chad Hennings: Okay, Troy. I want to start off by giving you a little background. I've begun many of the interviews in this book by sharing a story about when I stole some football cards as a kid and how it was a transformational moment for me because it was the first time I learned right from wrong. After hearing that story, Roger Staubach admitted to stealing something as a kid and so did Jason Garrett. The pressure is on now. Are you the third Cowboys quarterback to have stolen something when you were a young boy?

Troy Aikman (*laughing*): Well, I did unfortunately. Even before you told your story, I was thinking, *Oh, man.* I guess, shoot, my story happened when I was in first grade, so I was maybe six years old. I had a neighbor who was an older guy. He'd do woodshop and things and I'd go hang out with him in his shop. He was great. He was like a grandfather and he had a pocketknife that I always thought was really cool.

One day I was over there and it was on the table when I was leaving and I took it. When I got home I knew I had done wrong and I couldn't even bring myself to go in the house with it. We had a bunch of ivy on the side of the house and I threw it in there because I was just scared.

When my neighbor saw that it was missing, he went to my folks and they questioned me. I admitted it, and I had to dig around forever in the ivy trying to find the thing. I finally gave it back to him and I had to apologize. That was the last time I stole something. It was one of those deals where I thought, *Man, that's just not for me.* It was just so awkward and humbling.

Who are some of the people in your life, especially when you were younger, that you would say were mentors or influences of character?

For me it was always coaches. I respected my parents, but I didn't look to them as role models as much as I did coaches. I always had a lot of older friends too, and some of those guys would let me hang out with them and were guys I looked up to. Fortunately, they were all really good guys. They went on to be good people.

I want to jump to a pivotal moment in your life because I think it really illustrates the maturity that you showed at a young age. I'm talking about your decision to transfer from Oklahoma to UCLA.* That had to be a tough decision to make, leaving Barry Switzer and OU. Who did you rely on for advice and what was your thought process?

It was a hard decision primarily because I'd been dating a gal for five years through high school, and she was at OU as well. Knowing that I was leaving her and all the comforts of home was the most challenging thing. But I knew I had to leave in order to go where I wanted to go and to give myself a chance of fulfilling my dream of playing in the NFL. So that part of it was easy.

On the family side, my dad, gosh, as far back as I can remember, treated me like I was a grown man, so he just said, "Hey, whatever you want to do, go do it." It was kind of one of those deals. There wasn't a lot of handholding going on when I was looking to leave.

Considering the stakes, that's such an impressive decision to make for an eighteen- or nineteen-year-old. And it speaks to something I've mentioned in this book, which is that choosing the proper vector in life and committing to that is crucial. You chose early on to put your efforts into making it to the NFL and you didn't waiver, even when it might have been more comfortable to stay at Oklahoma. When did you first get it in your mind that you had a shot at playing in the pros?

Well, my dream from the time I was eight years old was to be a professional athlete. I thought it was going to be baseball at first, but then in high school and college it became football, so everything I did was with that in mind. That's really why I left OU. If I didn't have those dreams or if I didn't think I could realize them, I don't think I would have transferred.

Let's talk a little bit about the special relationship you had with your coach at UCLA, Terry Donahue. I know he was very much a mentor to you.

I've said it a lot, but I don't respect anybody more than I do him. He's an amazing guy. I just think the way that he carried himself with our team and the type of person he is even to this day is outstanding. He's got great integrity. He's got class, he's honest, he's tough, and he's firm.

All important aspects of character.

He's just the best. I think it's to the point where he's embarrassed to do anything in my company because I talk so much about what a great person he is. He's so humble, he says, "How am I supposed to live up to that?"

Where would you say you got your style of leadership? Was that self-taught or did you pick up stuff from other coaches and Coach Donahue?

I don't really know what my style is to be quite honest with you. I mean, you were around me. I tried to lead by example more than anything. I think that in order to be effective, you've got to be willing to do whatever it is you're expecting others to do. That would be my number one rule. You also have to know yourself.

Can you talk about that a little? How does self-awareness play a role in running the character of the team?

For me, I knew that I ran pretty hot when things weren't going the way I expected them to go, or people weren't taking things as seriously as I felt they needed to.

But in order to counter that, as a leader, I always felt that there's got to be a softer side. There's got to be an element that helps balance the days when I'm not real easy to be around. That's when I would make a point of putting my arm around guys and just say, "Hey, you're doing a great job and I really appreciate all that you're doing. Keep it up. Hey, don't worry about yesterday." It was that kind of stuff. But it was a constant balance for me because of my temperament. I had to work hard on the other side of it to not lose everybody.

That was strikingly similar to what Roger Staubach said in terms of leading by example. Both of you guys were men of action. When did you first realize that you had that leadership quality?

I think it was probably in junior high. It's a little different when you're young. I think as you get older, in football at least, the quarterback is immediately looked upon as the leader of the team whether he should be or shouldn't be. I don't know if that was necessarily the case when I was young. I never felt that anyone was looking more toward me when I was in Pop Warner as a quarterback than they were anyone else on the team. You know what I mean? We're all just doing what we do.

Junior high was when I began to realize that not everybody was as focused on being good as the next guy. I think that's when it began to reveal itself overall and to me in particular.

Any examples you can think of?

I remember going into my freshman year of high school I had an incident with an offensive lineman. Before practice started, me and some of the other guys were talking about what a great season we were going to have. Then we get into our two-a-days and our coach is working us pretty hard. It's hot and we're all tired, but this offensive lineman is complaining about all the extra running. He was supposed to be one of the leaders on the team and I was really upset about it. So I let him have it in front of the whole team.

I don't remember exactly what I said, stuff about how there's no room for complaining and that he had to get off his butt and run and do whatever. I think it was in those formative years that I started to recognize that even though everybody wants to win, not everybody really wants to put the time in or sacrifice the way you have to. So I realized I had to motivate people and drive them a little bit. I tended to do that, and I wasn't real sympathetic toward those I didn't think put in the time or effort.

Where do you think your inner driving force to succeed and win came from?

I think the biggest motivator for me was I was just fearful. I was afraid to fail. Especially when I got to the NFL and I was the first overall pick, I just didn't want to fail. I wanted my career to be looked upon as a success. I wanted to be viewed as a success. I didn't want to be one of those guys who came in and didn't live up to expectations. I think that was the motivator for me as much as anything.

But just as much as you were pushing other guys, you needed guys to push you. How did you go about surrounding yourself with individuals of character that could help you elevate your game and who would provide that relationship?

I've always wanted to be around people who made me better, more so now as I've gotten older. I got lucky because that Cowboys class I was drafted in was a great class. It was Daryl Johnston and [Tony] Tolbert and [Mark] Stepnoski. Immediately coming in, my roommates were Mark and DJ. It was the three of us right from the beginning. We were a lot alike; we all had goals to be good, and we were all willing to put in the time to make that happen. They were such hard workers, and that's how they were even when we came in as rookies.

We had guys like Step and DJ and a lot of those guys, but we also had some characters in that locker room. We had guys like Michael Irvin and Charles Haley always joking around. How were you able in that locker room to elevate everybody else, to pull everybody together that had different backgrounds to work toward one goal?

Well, as a specific example, people used to ask me all the time, "How do you get along with Michael?" I'd say, "Michael and I have the most unique relationship of any relationship I have. He and I are about as close as you can be. We never do anything together, but when we see each other, he'll come up and give me a kiss and hug. We love each other. We're almost like brothers, yet we couldn't be more different." And I can tell you that I think that relationship was really born out of the fact that at his core, like me, he just wanted to be great and he put in the work. There were so many guys on that team who were like that. Charles Haley, for as big of a goof as he his, wanted to be great. He was motivated by that and now he's in the Hall of Fame. For me, those were great years and those were great guys to be around.

When you talk about being willing to pay the price to be great, I think the flip side that I often saw was the people who had all the talent in the world but didn't have that drive. In pilot's terms, they had the mass and acceleration, but their vector was off so they crashed and burned. Sometimes those guys even wanted to be great, but they weren't willing to pay the price. Were there any strategies you employed to get the most out of those guys?

I think you see that at all levels. The guys who are good athletes continue to move up the chain, but their core doesn't change much. I think that for us, Jimmy Johnson was going to make it tough on those guys. Jimmy knew that most people don't mind losing. No one likes to lose, but for most people it doesn't really eat at them or hurt them. They're not that competitive. Jimmy decided that he was going to make life miserable for those guys and they weren't going to want to deal with him after a loss. If losing didn't bother the man, then he was going to make sure they didn't like being around him after a loss. That wasn't really his nature. I've gotten to know Jimmy really well here in the last ten, fifteen years. That guy wants to have more fun than anybody, so he really kind of had to put up that front.

When Barry Switzer came in, things got harder for me because I felt like rather than playing good cop to Jimmy's bad cop, I had to absorb the Jimmy role even more because nobody else would do it.

You spent a lot of time managing personalities, but at some point individuals have to take ownership of their trajectory. That's one of the things I talk about with my kids all the time, the aspect of ownership. I've tried to instill in them those aspects of character and integrity, of treating others appropriately, of selflessness, of humility, those things, but at some point, they have to own it for themselves. It can't be from me.

What we've been talking about in terms of some of the guys on those Cowboys teams is what I call functional character. That

includes resilience, work ethic, positive attitude, coachability, perseverance, those things. Whether it's sports or any other aspect of life, at some point in time, someone has to think to themselves, *I want to be great. I want to choose greatness and I'm willing to pay the price. It's part of who I am.* Do you remember when that moment in time was for you?

For me, there wasn't a light bulb moment. It was just how I was wired. Growing up, my dad would ask me all the time, "Hey, what do you want to be when you grow up?" I don't ever remember answering that question with anything other than I want to be a professional athlete. He would always follow that up with, "Well, you can be anything you want to be as long as you're willing to pay the price. There are things you got to do." He constantly preached that to me in those words, in those questions he would ask.

And also just being around him affected me. He was the hardest working guy I had seen and he demanded a lot from me, especially when we moved to Oklahoma. We were living on the farm and I had to manage all the expectations of chores and still try to fit in school and sports. To me that was how it always was.

For my daughters, we had a moment a few summers ago that I think is relevant here. I didn't want them sitting around all summer, so every day we'd go on a two-mile walk in the heat of the day. So we were walking one day, and we started talking about sports and their activities. Jordan's my oldest. She's thirteen now, she was probably ten at the time. I said, "The coach has been telling you to throw a hundred balls against the wall for lacrosse. I haven't seen you do it once."

I'm giving one of those talks, as we were walking, and I feel that nobody's walking behind me. I stop, I turn around, and both of my girls are fifteen yards behind. I said, "Hey," so they come up. Jordan almost has tears in her eyes. She says, "Dad, I don't want to disappoint you, but I'm not going to be a professional athlete." I just remember I felt like I had been punched.

I said, "Darling, there is no doubt in my mind that you're not going to be a professional athlete. I don't expect that for a minute, but that's not the point. The point isn't about you being a great athlete. The point is you're going to be something in life. I don't know what it's going to be. You're going to be a teacher. You're going to be a doctor. You're going to be a nurse. You're going to go to college. You're going to do something, and if you're going to be good at it, you've got to work at it. You've got to put in the time. You don't just show up and be good. You look at anybody who's good at whatever it is they do and think about all the people you look up to and you think, *Man, they're really good at that, or they're a good speaker, or they're good in math or whatever.* They work at it. It doesn't just happen." That was my lesson to them. I'll remember that moment for the rest of my life and I hope she will too.

That's a speech most professional athletes should give to their children. No matter what we do, they must feel like they're kind of burdened with that expectation. But what you said rings true. You have to work at anything you do. You were being a good

parent, but also showing good leadership, like I saw you do with the Cowboys. What would you say is the relationship between leadership and character?

That's a great question and I know it's one that's been discussed and written about for years and years and years. First, we need to define leadership, right? Leadership by definition is the ability to lead people. Simple. But how do people do that?

There have been a lot of bad people who have led others, who have moved people to do atrocious things. My definition of leadership is that you can't lead without integrity and character. The people who I've looked up to and the people who I have really viewed as great leaders have had great integrity and character because that's what I'm drawn to. Now maybe that's not true for everybody, but I believe you can't have one without the other. I believe if you have great integrity, just by its nature, you're a leader. I think people are drawn to that. Without integrity and without character, I just don't believe you can lead at all.

Now that we have some distance from our three Super Bowl championships, have you ever gone back in your mind and thought about your approach and either been impressed with yourself at a young age or discovered things you would have done differently?

I know we won a lot, but the truth is I never really knew how effective my approach was until after I retired. Now I'll hear other retired guys or college teammates tell stories about how I wouldn't let us take a play off or I'd do something in the huddle to take charge, and the truth is, I wasn't thinking about it in the moment.

It came natural to you.

I just didn't spend any time thinking about my style or whether what I was doing was the best way to do it. The way I was, to be honest, was just me. When I hear guys say nice things it does make me feel good, because I'm sure in quiet moments back then I wondered what the guys thought. Thinking about it now, I guess it worked for me because the guys knew it was pretty genuine. None of it was calculated, but since we're talking about it, I look back on some of my tantrums and some of the things I did when I was much younger and I'm really kind of embarrassed by it to be honest with you. I would be different I think if I were in that role today.

This leads to my last question: What would you tell the 25-year-old version of yourself if you ran into him today?

As I've gotten older, I've become a little more aware of what other people are dealing with. Jimmy and I were visiting a few years ago and were talking about this subject and he said to me, "Everybody has their bag of rocks. Everybody carries around their own bag of rocks. You never know what other people are dealing with on a day-to-day basis. Sometimes you can't see it."

When I was younger, I was all about winning. Every practice meant everything. Every game meant everything. I think I'd tell my younger self to be more tolerant of guys and learn a little bit more of their story and what might motivate them. I'd maybe tell myself to realize that they might have something going on that I don't know about. I think I was pretty good at recognizing what guys could handle in terms of criticism or praise, but I think taking the time to get to know why certain guys were the way they were would have been very helpful.

Empathy. That's very important. Thanks for your time, Troy.

Thanks, Chad.

*Troy Aikman was the starting quarterback at the University of Oklahoma. He broke his ankle during his junior season and the team went on to win the National Championship with another quarterback. Aikman chose to transfer to UCLA to continue his college career. He went 20-4 as UCLA's quarterback over two seasons and was a consensus All-American as a senior.

Epilogue

As I said in the introduction, my goal for this project was to walk readers through the life events and transformational moments that shaped the Forces of Character I've had the honor of knowing in my life.

Whether you have learned about mental toughness and the power of a positive attitude from Edie Eger; the symbiotic relationship between character and leadership from Roger Staubach and Troy Aikman; the imperative of choosing high-integrity people for your organization from Gregg Popovich; having the courage to stand by your decisions from Tom Henricks; or any other phenomenal piece of advice from the luminaries in this book, whatever your takeaway

Forces of Character

is, your journey to a life of character begins with your very next

decision.

The Forces of Character in this book have made a conscious choice to

try to live every day as their best possible self, to lift others to their

full potential and to elevate the performance of those around them.

The only question left is:

How do you choose to live?

ABOUT THE AUTHORS

Chad Hennings had a nine-year NFL career and won three Super Bowl Championships with the Dallas Cowboys. He also flew forty-five successful combat missions flying A-10 jets with the Air Force, and is one of the most decorated college football players in NCAA history. Chad has taken his message of character and leadership across the world at the invitation of some of the most distinguished audiences. He is the president of Hennings Management Corporation.

For more information on Chad Hennings, future *Forces of Character* projects and the C-Force Academy, visit: www.ForcesOfCharacter.com.

Follow Chad on Twitter: @ChadHennings

Jon Finkel is the author of *Heart Over Height* with 3x NBA Slam Dunk Champion Nate Robinson, as well as the hit fatherhood book, *The Dadvantage – Stay in Shape on No Sleep with No Time and No Equipment.* He authored *The Three Dollar Scholar – Awesome Advice for Acing Life's Major Decisions and Mindless Debates* as well. In the past he has written for *Men's Health, Men's Fitness, Muscle & Fitness, GQ, The New York Times,* Yahoo! Sports' *ThePostGame.com* and many more.

For more information on Jon, visit: www.JonFinkel.com

Follow Jon on Twitter: @Jon_Finkel